HOME FRONT
WWII in the Illinois Valley

By
R.G.Bluemer

©2005
Grand Village Press
134 Cleveland
Granville, IL 61326

M&D Printing
Henry, IL 61357

ISBN No. 09673680-6-5

No part of this book may be published without permission from the author.

A careful effort has been made to trace the ownership of all materials used in this work and to give proper credit to copyright owners. If any error or omission has been made, it is completely inadvertent. The publisher would like to make corrections in future editions provided that written notification is made to the publisher.
Grand Village Press, Granville, IL 61326

Front cover – Streator Canteen in WWII
Streatorland Historical Society.
Back cover – LST 1152, last Tank Landing Ship launched at Seneca shipyard.
US Navy photo.

This book is dedicated to Sgt. Glenn Bluemer WW II Veteran

Acknowledgements

A number of individuals provided personal accounts of events described in this work including Frank Rady, Ellsworth Zellmer, Jeno Bonucchi, Martha Yauch, Margarette Faletti, Sister Ann Rena Shinkey, Hazel Soberri, Ryan Cawley, Enis Barnato, and Harry Volant. Material on the Green River Ordnance Plant was generously shared by Duane Paulsen. John Shimkus contributed several cards and letters saved by the family during the war. The staff of the Streatorland Historical Society was especially helpful in locating little-known artifacts, photographs, and other resource material from the Streator area. Debbie Korn and Peggy Bluemer devoted long hours to proof reading the manuscript.

Contents

CHAPTER ONE
Day of Infamy

CHAPTER TWO
The Sleeping Giant Awakens

CHAPTER THREE
Another Year of Sacrifice

CHAPTER FOUR
Turning the Tide

CHAPTER FIVE
Final Push to Victory

Introduction

It has been over 60 years since WWII officially ended, and the survivors, both military and civilian, of that great conflict grow fewer in number with each passing year. Fortunately, many stories have been recorded of distant battlefields in Europe, Africa, and Asia. Unfortunately, it was not a war that ended future conflicts. In the 21st Century, American soldiers, sailors, marines, and airmen are sent to Europe and the Middle East to defend their country against a variety of threats. Whenever American servicemen are deployed, there are anxious friends, families, and loved ones left behind.

Using local newspaper accounts, personal interviews, and company records, this work focuses on those who remained in relative safety from the dangers of WWII and were eager to support the men and women of the armed forces in that conflict. This story is only a microcosm of one small section of the nation's civilian population that was united in an unprecedented commitment on farms and in factories to fill the needs of the military. It describes the generosity of social organizations, schools, and churches as they provided the home front support through scrap drives, bond sales, and volunteer services to achieve final victory. This is the story of the civilians of all ages who became the home front warriors.

No attempt has been made to include the name of every soldier, sailor, airman, and marine that left the safety of their homes, families, and friends in the Illinois Valley to defend the country. Nor will the reader find casualty lists or accounts of every recipient of a medal whether they were Purple Hearts or Bronze Stars. However, a few stories, based on published letters and newspaper interviews, are included to illustrate the experiences and sacrifices made by members of the armed forces and the impact those stories had on the home front.

CHAPTER ONE
Day of Infamy

The war in Europe had been going on since the Nazis invaded Poland in September 1939, so Americans were well aware of the spreading conflict. The Japanese expansion into China and Southeast Asia raised growing concerns among American political and military leaders, and limited action was taken to prepare for confrontation with the Japanese.

The growing rift between the Empire of Japan and the United States grew more obvious with each passing day in 1941. The Japanese high command knew that their plans for conquest depended on a surprise attack on the Pearl Harbor naval base at Oahu in the Hawaiian Islands. That action would have to be overwhelming to force the Americans to sue for peace.

When the Japanese attack was carried out on Sunday morning, Dec. 7, 1941, it indeed, appeared to be a decisive victory. Every battleship was either sunk or badly damaged. Thousands of American servicemen had been killed or wounded. But the extent of the damage was not such a disaster as to prevent the American forces from stopping the Japanese relentless drive through the South Pacific. Now, the Japanese army and navy not only had to deal with the American military, but also a united American civilian population, mobilized to a degree never before seen in the history of the United States.

At first, news of the surprise attack on the Hawaiian and Philippine Islands and Wake Island came only as news bulletins. The complete story of the devastation and loss of lives would not be released for weeks or even months following the attacks. But even limited reports spurred local officials into action.

The local press responded the next day. An editorial in the LaSalle *Daily Post-Tribune* on Dec. 8 summed up what many civilians knew in their hearts. It read in part, "If it is to be war – let's not fool around about it. Let's not fool ourselves – every man woman, and child will be in it. We know that many of the young men will be direct participants – will do the actual fighting. We know that the rest of us – those back home will pay the bills, if not one way, in another." An editorial in the Ottawa *Republican Times* defiantly proclaimed, "Gangster Japan has asked for it, and gangster Japan shall have it, from an America united as it seldom has been in its history."

City officials responded as well. In Oglesby, Mayor Frank Moyle made a motion at the Dec. 8 city council meeting that the city should adopt the slogan "V-For Victory." In addition, Moyle recommended the construction of a four-foot wooden "V" painted white; installed in front of the Oglesby city hall; and illuminated at night until final victory was achieved. In the meantime, a small "V" sign was installed over the door to city hall. After the meeting, Oglesby Commissioner J.L. Rock said, "Now we will go in there and lick the daylights out of those Japs."

Pearl Harbor under attack on Dec. 7, 1941. US Navy photo.

LaSalle Mayor H. M. Orr, expressed the feelings of many saying, "This cowardly act that has brought about the destruction of American lives and property will solidify our nation. This solidarity will spell 'doomsday' for the Japanese in the very near future." Other community leaders expressing indignation included M.J. Faletti, chairman of the local selective service board, Terrance S. Martin, the Tri-City Red Cross Service Officer, and Frank Spayer, commander of the Romulus Meehan American Legion Post.

A statement by Stuart Duncan, President of the LaSalle State Bank, was a reflection of attitude throughout the Illinois Valley. "The treacherous act on the part of Japan had the effect of uniting the people of the United States of America, and they will see this achieved to the finish."

According to the *Mendota Reporter*, residents barely left their radios Sunday afternoon and evening when the news of the attack by Japan was heard. Several Mendota servicemen were members of the fleet and aviation groups on Oahu. There were serious concerns for Ensign John J. Westerman, a member of the crew of the *USS Maryland*. The paper went on to point out that about 100 young men from Mendota were already in the service, and others would soon be drafted.

War production in Mendota would likely be increased with some of the government contracts going to the Conkey Co. An army officer was sent to the plant to assist in the implementation of unspecified war production, and security at the plant was immediately tightened to prevent sabotage. Identification buttons would be issued to all employees in the near future. Other citizens organized into a civilian defense committee to assist the police and fire departments, as well as medical organizations "in case of a disaster."

Security was also tightened in the Streator railroad yards. The Santa Fe RR sent extra guards to patrol the Vermillion River railroad bridge.

For the average citizen, news of the Pearl Harbor attack heightened concerns for loved ones overseas. Mrs. Leon Harris, who was Hawaiian-born and wife of the pastor of St. Paul's Episcopal church in LaSalle, expressed concern about her mother, grandmother, brother, and three sisters in Honolulu.

Communication with the islands after the attack was spotty at best. Five families in Spring Valley had sons stationed at Hickam Field, one of the targets of the Japanese on Dec. 7th. A transoceanic phone call on Tuesday, Dec. 9th, took two hours to complete, but it brought brief and reassuring news that the young men, Thurman Dwyre, Leonard Gailis, John Kerulis, Robert Blum, and Felix Lukosus, were "all right." The conversation was strictly limited by security restrictions. There could be no exchange of information regarding the military situation on Oahu. Specific details about the soldiers' experience that fateful day would not be revealed until months later. However, two days later Mr. and Mrs. Allen Dwyre were notified that their son had been wounded in the attack on Dec. 7th. Sgt. Dwyre and his friend, Bob Blum of Webster Park, had been training in aviation. Both men along with Leonard Gailis were scheduled to return to the States just before the Pearl Harbor attack.

One of the last letters Dwyre had written was on Nov. 25 to Glenn Sitterly, an aviator and president of Western Sand and Gravel. He said that he was looking forward to receiving his orders. Dwyre added that Cpl. Kerulis was "working day and night" as an engineer on B-18's "to keep 'em flying."

Hickam Field, Pearl Harbor, P-26's and B-18's on the flight line, Jan. 1940.
US Navy photo.

All of the Spring Valley boys were at Hickam Field during the attack, and loved ones waited anxiously for word of their safety. The mail had to get past the censors. Letters from Dwyre and Blum finally arrived in Spring Valley later in December. Blum said that Dwyre and Lukosus were fine although they were both wounded in the attack. Although a bomb exploded only 20 feet from his position, Blum was unhurt. He said that morale was high and "everybody wants to get the Japs." Several months later, all of them, except Kerulis, who remained in the Hawaiian Islands, were sent back to California for additional training.

One young man from Ottawa, Kenneth Engel, was also stationed at Hickam Field during the attack. After finishing training at Chanute Field at Rantoul, he received orders to report to Hawaii in November 1941. Engel was not listed as a casualty.

Months after the attack on Pearl Harbor, the government finally released photos of the damage that Sunday morning such as this one of a hanger at Hickam Field. US Navy photo.

Anxious parents continued to wait for news from the sons serving abroad. On Dec. 15, the LaSalle *Post-Tribune* printed the story and photo (left) of the first war-related fatality from the area, Leo Cotner, a 17-year old sailor from Leonore. He had enlisted in March 1941 and was stationed with his brother, Francis, at Pearl Harbor. Initial details were lacking, but the navy finally reported that Cotner was killed in the attack on the *USS Nevada*. Francis, who had gone below to get some water for the gun crew was wounded in the explosion that killed his brother.

USS Nevada was able to get underway after being bombed on Dec. 7th but was beached to make sure that the channel would not be blocked. US Navy photo.

The following day, the newspaper reported another fatality. The navy had informed Mr. and Mrs. J.R. Smith of Arlington that their son, Thomas Dudley Smith, who enlisted on his 17th birthday, had been killed on Dec. 9, while on duty in the Pacific. The family scheduled a memorial mass at St. Patrick's Church in Arlington. The family's grief was turned to joy, a few weeks later. On New Year's Eve, the Navy Department sent another telegram informing the family that "Dudley," who had attended Hall H.S., wasn't killed after all. He was safe.

Unfortunately, Western Union continued to deliver notifications bearing the sad refrain "regrets to inform you" to other families. Another local fatality at Pearl Harbor was Gunner's  Mate Thomas Powell. The L-P High School track star left in his junior year to enlist in the navy. He was the first casualty from Oglesby. Although the information received was not specific as to the cause of the young sailor's death, it was known that he had been serving aboard the *USS Arizona*. (Photo- GM Thomas Powell - Oglesby Library). Cpl. James McCarrens, a Marine from Ottawa, was also assigned to the *Arizona*. There was no immediate information on whether he had survived the attack, but some time later, it was reported that he had been killed. Mrs. Chester Sherman of rural Ottawa also learned that her son, S3c Herman O. Koeppe, was missing-in-action. The navy later reported that he had also died as a result of the attack on the *USS Arizona*.

USS Arizona, Dec. 7, 1941, U.S. Navy photo.

The first reported casualty from Peru was FC3c Adolph John Loebach, who was assigned to the battleship *USS Oklahoma*, which was lost at Pearl Harbor. The 21-year old had attended L-P high school for three years and later worked for the National Sheet Metal Co. in Peru before enlisting. The Navy Department did not indicate if Loebach was on the ship when it was sunk. The War Department telegram only informed his father, Henry Loebach Jr., that his son was "missing-in-action." In February, a memorial mass was celebrated at St. Mary's Catholic Church in Peru. The Peru American Legion provided an honor guard.

Telegrams containing similar news were received throughout the Illinois Valley. The Halterman family of Ottawa, was informed that their 20-year old son, Robert, was missing. The son of Bertha Denny, Arthur Denny, had enlisted with Halterman on Dec. 27, 1939 and was also on the *Oklahoma*. Mrs. Anne Novak of Streator was also concerned about her son, Michael, who was also assigned to the *Oklahoma*.

USS Oklahoma capsized at Pearl Harbor. Dec. 7, 1941. U.S. Navy photo.

The fate of the *USS Hulbert* (AVP-60) was of special interest to the family of Seaman Tom Weitzel who was assigned to the seaplane tender when the Sunday morning attack was unleashed at Pearl Harbor. When the Navy Department finally released the full details of the attack, the Weitzel family learned that the crew had shot down one Japanese torpedo plane and hit several more enemy planes without suffering any casualties.

When information was received that the *USS West Virginia* was sunk by six torpedoes and two bombs, the word spread that Henry "Hank" Ellerbrock from Ladd was aboard. Fortunately, he survived the attack.

One of the numerous destroyers at Pearl Harbor was the *USS McCall*. Carroll Rawling, son of Mrs. Elmer Munson of 1445 Birchlawn Pl., Ottawa, had been assigned to the ship, and there was no news from the sailor. When the navy finally reported on the status of the ship, it was learned that, on Dec. 7, the *USS McCall* was not at Pearl Harbor, but rather was screening for the *USS Enterprise* as the ships were returning to Oahu from Wake Island.

USS McCall. US Navy photo.

Many other families from Ottawa had loved ones stationed at bases in the Pacific threatened by the Japanese advance. Fred Prichard and his wife had been concerned for some time about their son, Capt. Lawrence Prichard, who had been stationed at Zamboanga in the Philippines. Captain Prichard's wife had been evacuated several months before the Japanese attack. Mr. and Mrs. Arthur Finch of Grand Ridge were also troubled by the news of the Japanese aggression in the Pacific. Although their sons were not based at Pearl Harbor, their oldest boy, Leroy, was stationed on Samoa, and his younger brother, Louis, was at the Cavite naval base near Manila. Also stationed at Cavite was Clarence Shumaker, son of Mr. and Mrs. K.F. Shumaker of 708 Chestnut Street, Ottawa.

Andrew Sagi, whose family lived at 1027 Sycamore St. Ottawa, was a radio operator on the *USS Tutuila*, which had been routinely patrolling the inland rivers of China. It was dangerous work. A similar river patrol boat, *USS Panay*, was sunk by the Japanese on Dec. 27, 1937. The *Tutuila* had also come under attack by the Japanese months earlier while patrolling the Yangtze River near Chungking. Unknown to the folks back home, before the Dec. 7th attack, the crew was flown to the Philippines, and the boat was turned over to the Nationalist Chinese government.

The *USS Tutuila* (PR-4) was photographed on the Yangtze River. US Navy photo.

While the Japanese attack was considered a major blow to America's battleship force in the Pacific, the aircraft carriers were out on patrol on Dec. 7th. The *USS Saratoga* had just been refitted and on Dec. 7th had just arrived in San Diego. That came as good news for the Lockwood family in Ottawa. Their son, Ensign James Lockwood, an Annapolis graduate, was assigned to the *Saratoga*. Worries continued however, because the carrier immediately departed on Dec. 8 to link up with the carriers *USS Lexington* and *USS Enterprise* to search for the Japanese fleet.

USS Saratoga, 1942. US Navy photo.

The spirit of the citizens, although shaken by fragmentary news reports, was not deterred from acts of generosity to the hundreds of servicemen in training camps and bases across the country and around the world. The LaSalle American Legion and

Women's Auxiliary quickly went to work organizing a "Smokes-for-Yanks" program. They planned to send packages of 100 cigarettes, along with pies and cookies, to every serviceman from the area. Gift packages containing cigarettes, cookies, and candy from the LaSalle American Legion and Women's Auxiliary were gratefully acknowledged. Ed Volk in the Army Air Corps in Victoria, TX; Frank Vogrine at Sheppard Field, TX; Leonard Dudek at Ft. Eustis, VA; Frank Udvance at Kessler Field MI.; and Ignatius Vicare at Ft. Sill, OK were just a few of the LaSalle men who wrote letters of appreciation to the American Legion for its generosity.

In Streator, Capt. Fred Mills, commander of Co. F of the Illinois Reserve Militia, expressed hope that enlistments in his unit would quickly increase from 40 members to the maximum of 64. That limitation was changed by the end of December so that the Streator unit could be increased to 90. The reserve unit would eventually be used to guard roads and bridges during black-out drills.

In the weeks after the attack, public-spirited citizens stepped forward to volunteer their services. Fred Wagner, a ham radio operator from Mendota, offered to make his radio transmitter available to the Mendota Defense Organization to relay messages overseas. At that time, the government allowed each city to have one transmitter for such purposes. Ted Coppin, a Streator businessman and licensed pilot, applied for assignment to the Civil Air Patrol, which helped with a variety of Civil Defense duties.

There was an immediate need for additional men to fill the ranks of the Army Air Corps. Turn Hall in Peru was the scene of increased activity on Dec. 11, when an army aviation cadet examination board was established. Four army officers together with eight enlisted men moved into the American Legion rooms to recruit men for positions such as aviation cadets, aeronautical engineers, communications specialists, and navigation bombardiers. Normally, enlistees signed up for three years and nine months, but the declaration of war with Japan changed that. Now, enlistees signed up for the duration of hostilities. Those meeting the age requirements (20-26), and passing the physical and training exams, would graduate as staff sergeant pilots. Those enlistees with two years of college experience did not have to take the educational exams. High school graduates and those with one year of college courses would be exempted from taking subjects for which they had credit. Although only single men were traditionally accepted, married applicants could enlist if their spouses would sign waivers not holding the government responsible for the care of the wives.

The military programs were exclusively a man's world for some time. Gladys Haupt, an 18 year old female from Peru, who worked at Westclox, tried to enlist in the aviation cadet program but was rejected even though she had pilot training. However, the officers on the panel did praise her for her "patriotic spirit."

The examining board met again on Dec. 18 and enlisted Arnold J. Wilson, a sales engineer for Westclox. Wilson would be going first to a 10-week program at a replacement training center. That would be followed with 15 weeks of navigation training. The final training would involve additional classes in bombardier school. Upon graduation, graduates were commissioned as second lieutenants in the Army Air Corps.

Civic groups offered whatever help they thought might be needed. The Tri-City Chamber of Commerce, headed by Frank Lang, sent out inquiries to defense industries seeking to fill the empty Peru Wheel factory. In Lang's opinion, the vacant buildings would be suitable for the production of tanks. Oglesby Mayor Moyle recommended the use of the reading and recreation rooms in the Dickinson Field House for the needs of the Red Cross even if it meant the elimination of current programs.

The Japanese general staff knew that the attack on Pearl Harbor had to be decisive to pressure the Americans to sue to peace. They also knew that failure to achieve that goal would only stir a sleeping giant. The American home front reaction was something that the Japanese woefully underestimated. The giant was about to waken.

CHAPTER TWO
The Sleeping Giant Awakens

The home front effort to support the war became more than symbolic platitudes. Concrete action finally began to unfold. One of the first actions required by the federal government was the rationing of tires. With the Japanese in control of the rubber plantations of Southeast Asia, it was quickly apparent that civilians would be allotted only a fraction of the tires and inner tubes that normally would be available at local dealers. In LaSalle County, the job of county rationing director went to A.D. Jobst. Three other Ottawans, Richard Knott, Olive Dunham, and Burton Palmer, were also given positions on the rationing board. Scott E. Weller was assigned as a special agent for the board.

The applicants for the new tires and inner tubes had to fill out applications at the rationing board office in the Hotel Kaskaskia. Each applicant had to specify the exact vehicle that would be fitted with the tires as well as the intended use of the vehicle. Weller said that it would be a waste of time to apply if the individual was not clearly eligible to buy tubes or tires. Regulations specified that priority would be given to those in the medical profession, such as doctors, surgeons, visiting nurses, and veterinarians. Some individuals were in luck if they needed obsolete tire sizes or sought to buy recapped tires since they were not regulated. Those tires were easily procured.

Each month, counties would be allotted a certain number of tires and inner tubes. For example, in January 1942, LaSalle County had a quota for the month of 74 tires (a.k.a. casings) and 62 inner tubes for automobiles, light trucks, and motorcycles. The quota for heavier trucks was about three times that number. Bureau County was only allotted 31 tires and 26 tubes for the lighter vehicles and trucks. Putnam County's quota was a meager 4 tires and 3 inner tubes. One of the additional restrictions was that no county rationing board could dispense more than 25 percent of its allotment in any one week. The quotas would vary each month as determined by military necessities. Each state would also retain eight percent of its monthly quota to make adjustments.

Since tires were going to be very hard to obtain in Putnam County, the tire rationing board consisting of Fred Gallaher, A.F. Nelson, and C.O. Read, met at the court house on Jan. 10 to discuss questions about the system. The owners of six service stations in the county, I.F. Stonier and J.A. Wallace (Granville), Vivian Colby (Hennepin), Lloyd Koehler (McNabb), Charles Johnston (Magnolia), and George Morehouse (Putnam), were going to check to make sure that an applicant for a replacement tire really needed one.

The Federal Price Administrator, John C. Weigel, tried to reassure those who had to commute to their jobs. He said, "There is no need for people to get panicky. The fact that a rationing plan is going into effect on Jan. 5 doesn't mean that everyone is going to get a flat tire at 12:01 a.m. on Jan. 5."

Being an agricultural area, farmers in the Illinois Valley were quite concerned over the availability of finding replacement tires for tractors and other farm vehicles. Weigel suggested that farmers might consider the possibility of "putting steel wheels back on many tractors and farm implements, which have been converted for the use of rubber tires."

One immediate effect of the tire rationing program was the requirement for an inventory of tires in stock by local dealers. Sheriff E.J. Welter contacted all dealers in LaSalle through local police departments to insure that the Jan. 3 deadline for inventories was met on time.

It was soon apparent that the shortage of natural rubber was going to have a major impact on the availability of tires and inner tubes. Henry Pope Jr. the state tire rationing administrator, soon forecast slashes in quotas for February. All of LaSalle County would only be allotted 60 tires for passenger cars. Bureau County residents also faced a similar reduction down to 25 tires, and Putnam County would only be allotted 3 tires. Applicants who wanted to purchase tires were informed by Ed Kolowski, chairman of the Tri-City rationing board, exactly what would be necessary. All applicants had to appear in person at city hall before board secretary Sgt. Jim Callahan to answer specific questions. Some of the first applicants included trucking companies such as H.J. Tobler and the Oglesby Motor Transportation Co.

A report by the rationing board on the distribution of tires and tubes was released in March. The police department in Oglesby was allotted two tires and two inner tubes. Peru was allowed to purchase four inner tubes for its ambulance. Certificates for obsolete tires were picked up by Barclay Wallace of Troy Grove and E.G. Booth of Meriden. Lewis Dewey and Joe Funfsinn of Mendota picked up certificates to purchase tires for their tractors and farm equipment. Other tire purchase certificates went to various trucking outfits.

The U.S. District Attorney's office also notified LaSalle Police Chief Peter Walloch that new regulations were in effect regarding aliens from Germany, Japan, and Italy. Effective Jan. 5, all broadcasting equipment, shortwave radios, cameras, and firearms owned by those individuals had to be surrendered to the police. If any of those items were later found in the possession of an enemy alien, the prohibited article would be confiscated, and the person would be arrested. Local police would provide a receipt for all illegal items, which would be returned after the war.

As the deadline approached, and additional warnings were published in the local papers, only a few items were turned over to the authorities. Three persons of Italian descent complied by turning in a total of three shotguns and one revolver.

Streator also had a large population of Germans and Italians. Several guns and cameras were turned over to the police, but no shortwave radios were confiscated.

Getting a jump on military training was an initiative carried out by the Oglesby American Legion Post. Meetings were held at the Washington school gym. New draft laws allowed fathers and sons to join the military together if the son's age is only slightly below the 20 year old requirement. Ed Schmitz and his son, Jack, showed up at the training meeting along with seven others. Two men, who had been recently discharged having reached age 28, offered to help with the training.

In mid-January, The LaSalle-Peru Elks decided to set up a committee to implement at the local level the national Elks program called "Keep 'Em Flying." The basic idea of the program was to provide a "refresher course" for men 20-27 who were interested in taking the aptitude test for the Army Air Corps as

Flying Cadets, navigators, or bombardiers. Five local men had expressed interest in such a course. If there were fewer than 20 men enrolled locally, a plan was in place to form a larger group by combining enrollments with those candidates sponsored by the Elks of Ottawa. Later in the year, the Elks Lodge in Mendota offered to help recruit volunteers for the Seabees and the Army Construction Engineers. The Elks War Committee, chaired by O.J. Elinger, agreed to distribute literature and posters to help the army and navy in finding men for construction specialties.

It appeared that everyone wanted to do something to help the troops. Besides, cigarettes, cookies, and candy, a national effort to collect books was started by the National Library Association, the Red Cross and the United Service Organization (USO). The "Victory Book Campaign," had as its goal the collection and distribution of donated books to servicemen. The program officially kicked off on Jan. 15. Tessie Yopp, the LaSalle librarian, was in charge. Evelyn Ball (Peru), Vivian Reber (Oglesby), and Maysel Baker (L-P Township), assisted in the Tri-Cities. In Putnam County, Virginia Jones, county librarian, and the eight local directors, Mrs. Sam Kessler, Ann Cioni, Enis Silverstrini, Mrs. Lucretia Franklin, Mrs. George Mathis, Mrs. Charles Read, Bess Davidson, and Carolyn Larsen, sought to reach a goal of 5,280 books. Helping the librarians were the Boy Scouts, PTA, Red Cross, and a variety of church and service clubs. The national goal was to collect ten million books for men of the armed forces and merchant marine.

A rendition of the "Books for Buddies" poster by C.B. Falls was printed in the LaSalle *Post-Tribune* on Jan. 12, 1942.

The Boy Scouts of the Starved Rock Area Council also participated in a new "Air Scout" program developed at the national level. Three steps were added to the traditional scouting program. These involved the institution of three levels of expertise beginning with "Air Scout Observer," progressing to "Air Scout Technician," and culminating with "Air Scout Craftsman."

The services of the Boy Scouts in Peru were offered to the Peru city council by Carl Struever, Junior Asst. Scoutmaster and Charles Bleneman, Scoutmaster of Troop 4. Bleneman suggested that the boys could collect paper, scrap metal, and rubber, and if needed, serve as messengers. He said, "We are willing to do anything the Boy Scouts may be called upon to perform."

Girl Scouts were not left out of the service effort. Mary Stevenson came down from Chicago to address troop leaders at the LaSalle Lutheran church in February. She said, "When war came, the Girl Scouts were prepared. For more than a year before hostilities began, the Girl Scouts had been intensifying activities which would prove of special use should an emergency arise." She pointed to their skills in nursing, first aid, and community service. Stevenson also noted the activities of St. Hyacinth's troop led by Miss Emily Jasiek. Miss Hilda Schoening of LaSalle and Miss Francis Sikora of Peru assumed the duties of chairpersons of a leadership association. When one member of the audience complained that everyone was busy with defense work, Stevenson retorted, "Girl Scouting is defense work." She added that since 1940, through their service bureau, Girl Scouts had given thousands of hours of volunteer work to the Red Cross, area hospitals, and welfare groups. Now that war had been declared, she said, the Girl Scouts were planning even more activities.

Local schools were also involved in a variety of programs to support the war effort. Dr. Frank Jensen, Superintendent of LaSalle-Peru H.S. and L-P-O Jr. College, reported to the board of education plans to have the sale of national defense stamps in 10, 25, and 50-cent denominations in the school book store. He also explained that an air raid drill was planned for Jan. 8, and plans were underway for faculty assistance with the registration for the draft on Feb. 16. Virtually every school building was going to be used for the registration of men between 20 and 45. Registration sites included L-P High School and the Washington, Lincoln, and Jefferson schools in LaSalle, the Roosevelt, Central, and McKinley schools in Peru, and the Washington and Lincoln schools in Oglesby. In addition, Jensen noted that there was a 100 percent enrollment by faculty and students in the Red Cross.

On Jan 8, the Washington and Lincoln schools in Oglesby also conducted their first air raid drill. Students were taught to stay away from windows in case of a real attack. It was planned to have similar practice air raids every week.

Since skill as a Morse code operator was deemed both essential to the needs of the military and a real advantage to men entering the military, the American Legion in Oglesby decided to offer courses in code recognition and transmission and established an aviation ground school. So, every Thursday night, licensed instructors taught code at the Thomas Larkin Post.

The Peru Legionnaires took a similar course of action. Since Morse code was used throughout the military, the men decided to simply teach Army draftees the basics of sending and receiving code without going into the specifics of radio theory. Earl Seaton was named to take charge of the committee running the program on Wednesday nights at Turn Hall in Peru. Other members of the committee included Herbert Bekermeier, Steve Romanowski, George Keith, and Walter Eich. Seaton asked that anyone having old headsets or telegraph keys loan them to the post. Meetings began on Jan 21.

The Radio Code School: George Keith, chief instructor seated next to typist; standing in back are Herb Bekermeier, Earl Seaton, and Steve Romanowski. Others included Leo Schmidt & Bob Ball. Westclox photo, *Tick Talk magazine.*

The Oglesby Booster Club took on the responsibility for a code communication project and a ground school for prospective fliers. George Shields, president of the club, appointed Frank Moyle Jr., who was a licensed pilot, as the instructor for the ground school of the air. Lawrence McCann was the instructor for the Morse code classes.

The War Department was in desperate need of experienced radio operators and actively sought out those with telegraphy experience as well as those who had training in physics or electrical engineering. Single men between the ages of 21 and 36 were being commissioned in the army signal corps, and the navy was offering commissions ranging from ensign to lieutenant commander for qualified applicants.

While various groups worked to provide for anticipated needs of the military, there was still a need to expand war production facilities. There was factory space available locally. Peru Wheel Co. operations had been absorbed by the Electric Wheel Co. in Quincy, IL and Apollo Metal Works had moved operations to Chicago. So, there were two major facilities standing empty. Mayor Orr contacted Senator Brooks to offer their use in war production. There would be plenty of government work down the road, and LaSalle was anxious to vie for the contracts.

Many Westclox workers enlisted or were drafted for the armed forces following the Pearl Harbor attack. In January 1942, the company illustrated its concern for the men by promising four week's pay, a year's premium for the government's insurance plan, and a promise to reinstate the men in their jobs with full seniority benefits when they returned from military duty.

In Oglesby, a mass meeting was held on Jan. 14 at the Washington School to facilitate the hiring of additional women for the new Eicor Inc. plant on West Walnut Street. Increasing defense orders required an expansion of Eicor's capacity to manufacture electrical motors.

Ad reprinted from Mar. 21, 1942 edition of LaSalle *Post Tribune*.

A temporary factory headquarters with 41 employees was set up in the Lorenzetti building on East Walnut. Another 35-40 workers would be needed in the expanded facility.

War production began to have an impact in Ottawa at Libbey-Owens-Ford Glass Co. Their Toledo, Ohio office announced that the Ottawa plant had received a "machine shop job" that would begin in February. D.H. Goodwillie, the executive vice president, stated, "We hope this will be one of many defense orders for the Ottawa factory." It was good news for L-O-F workers who had been laid off when the laminating line had been shut down in December after officials in Washington decided that civilian automobile production would be halted. The previous year, 1600 workers had jobs at the plant. Since that time, the work force had shrunk to 100.

War materials were not cheap, and the cost to maintain the growing military forces gave rise to a variety of government loan programs. In its *Tick Talk* monthly magazine, Westclox workers were urged to buy as many bonds as possible through payroll deductions. It pointed out that one 10¢ defense stamp would pay for five bullets. Another 25¢ in stamps could pay for a soldier's mess kit, and $1.50 in stamps would cover the cost of a first aid kit. Everyone was encouraged to contribute financially to the war effort.

Ad reprinted from the LaSalle *Daily Post-Tribune*, Jan. 30, 1942.

Children of all ages were involved in supporting the war – especially at school. St. Hyacinth's Catholic School in LaSalle used the theme of "Victory" in a patriotic program presented at the end of January. The program opened with the "Victory March" led by pupils carrying Polish and American flags with the Boy Scouts rendering a martial drumbeat. A student dressed as Uncle Sam was followed by four girls in Red Cross uniforms. Everyone stood for the Pledge of Allegiance and joined in singing "God Bless America." Students marched down the aisle in the victory march and placed a coin in boxes held by the Red Cross girls while everyone sang "Remember Pearl Harbor." The 286 pupils each contributed a dime for the Red Cross War Relief fund in LaSalle. The finale consisted of a Polish patriotic song and the "Star Spangled Banner." The $28.67 collected was a small amount in the total scheme of things, but, coupled with the stirring program, it showed in one small way, the unity that was sweeping the nation.

    Patriotic songs and martial music had their place, but there was a more ominous side to war. The Peru Civil Defense Council called a meeting on Feb. 3 to review local preparedness for possible acts of sabotage. Herbert Bekermeier, chairman of the committee acknowledged, "We have quite a task ahead of us even though we have not had the anxiety which prevails on both coasts. As far as the possibility of bombing raids in the central west is concerned, that idea is pretty far-fetched. Our most serious worry is sabotage." The commander of the Peru American Legion said that 195 members were ready to serve in protecting local factories. An auxiliary police force and fire fighters unit was also being organized. Even the local postal workers promised their cooperation. A few months later, Peru City Clerk Francis Klug sent out 2,500 invitations seeking volunteers for the Air Observation Service, which had already been established in the coastal areas.

    Although the possibility of an air raid seemed remote, the schools held scheduled air raid alerts. During the initial practice at L-P High School, the rooms were cleared on the vulnerable top floor, and everyone lined up in double rows in the first and second floor corridors within two minutes. Those students in the gym or swim classes were also sent to protected areas of the building. Each teacher was designated as an air raid warden responsible for the safety of their students. To add realism to the alerts, it was planned to have unannounced drills later in the month.

    The L-P vocational classes were involved in a nationwide project to construct model airplanes for use by the army and navy in training military and civil defense airplane spotters. Students were given the task of building 300 model airplanes. This was part of the state's quota of 30,000 models. Blueprints and drawings for the planes would be sent to the school, which would supply the wood and glue for the 6 sets of 50 different models of American and Axis planes. The $100 cost for the project was not in the school budget so a model plane fund was established for those wishing to make a donation. All of the students in the manual training classes would participate in the construction. All other shop projects would be put on hold until the quota was filled. Other students were asked to help out after school.

The military draft was quickly instituted, and quotas were set for even the smallest communities. Registration for the Selective Service was held in Putnam County on Feb 16. A total of 252 men signed up at the four high schools in Granville, Hennepin, McNabb, and Senachwine. The quota of men called in the Putnam County would be small compared to other counties.

It was a sobering and tearful occasion when the first large contingent of draftees left LaSalle on Feb. 13, 1942. Hundreds of friends and relatives gathered at city hall to hear Michael Faletti, chairman of the local draft board, praise the men for their readiness to serve their country. After the farewell speeches, Arthur Querciagrossa and Ervin Barber took charge of boarding the men on the 8 a.m. bus to Camp Grant in Rockford.

A week later, 23 more draftees would take the same journey. Such departures soon became commonplace, but the *Post-Tribune* had a photographer on hand to record each event for the front page of its next edition.

By March 1942, hundreds of men from the Illinois Valley had departed for military training camps or were already serving at military bases around the world. To honor those men, the state of Illinois issued Silver Star emblems for display in the windows of the families who had men in the service. The motto was "Our Home Has Contributed." The first of the emblems was issued to the family of Bert Odekirk at

414 River St. in LaSalle. Another one was provided to Frank Godawa, whose brother was serving at Camp Forrest, TN. A third Silver Star emblem went to the family of Lt. Albert Knauf, who was serving in the Army Air Corps. Hundreds of the emblems were available at the Daily Post-Tribune office in LaSalle.

By late February, Peru joined other cities in the planning stages for the planting of Victory gardens in the spring. Peru's mayor, Al Hasse, decided to offer residents the opportunity to plant gardens on small plots of the 35 acres of city-owned land on the south side of the Illinois River. A few individuals had been cultivating this land during the Depression, but in the years leading up to Dec. 7th, not many people had bothered to plant private gardens. Although the bottomland was inundated by high water, it was expected that the river level would drop, so it was time to develop a plan to divide the land into small parcels.

Later in the year, Dave Malone and Joe Cavaletto, who were in charge of the victory garden project in Oglesby, came up with the idea of awarding prizes for the best vegetable garden. In addition, they decided that flower gardens should be a separate category in awarding prizes. Gardens would have to have the flowers planted in a "V" for victory to be eligible for an award.

The Illinois Valley Brewers and Distributors Assn. ran this ad in the Feb. 21, 1942 edition of the LaSalle *Daily Post-Tribune* to explain their cooperation with the demands of the federal government to conserve truck, gas, oil, and other materials needed by the armed forces. Trucks from Bernardi's, Bonucci's Wholesale Liquor, Tino DeFillipi's Pabst Distributing, Star Union, Peru Products, and other distributors in the association would cease making deliveries on Thursdays, Sundays, and Holidays.

Spring Valley authorities also took an interest in finding suitable land for victory gardens. Dr. George Sutton, chairman of the committee charged with the task, addressed a meeting at city hall on Mar. 5. He began by reading a letter from the State Department stating that virtually all trains would be used to transport war materials, not produce, and it was expedient for communities to raise as many fresh vegetables as possible. Sutton warned that this plan should not cause hysteria as it did in WWI when residents were digging up their front yards to plant a garden. He also stated that Spring Valley would not have a community garden but rather encouraged each family to take care of their own small plot. It would be the committee's job to survey the city to determine the potential number of garden plots.

This ad for defense bonds appeared in the Feb. 28, 1942 edition of the LaSalle *Daily Post-Tribune* not only encouraged more people to buy bonds and pointed out that the liquor tax of $1.3 billion collected across the country was helping to build American bombers.

Railroad transportation was a major issue facing all of the towns along the Rock Island tracks from Joliet to Bureau. In mid-February, the Rock Island filed a petition to discontinue service on the daily westbound 11:16 a.m. passenger train and the daily 4:40 a.m. eastbound train No. 212, and the No. 214 that operated only on Sundays at 7:56 a.m. An appeal was filed with the Commerce Commission to emphasize the importance of the Rock Island service to Spring Valley. Attorney Paul Perona made a strong case for the community in Springfield explaining, "The trains are the lifeblood of the city so far as mail and express shipments are concerned." The *Spring Valley Gazette* reported on Mar. 19 that the Rock Island would continue to operate the trains.

News and photographs of the Pearl Harbor attack were slowly released to home front. The few telegrams that were received by local families never contained any specifics. Those who suffered wounds were treated in Hawaiian hospitals before being shipped back to California and eventually to their homes. It was at that point that the public received eyewitness accounts of the tragedy. S1c Glenn Berghefer, 20, a sailor on the cruiser *USS Helena* was one of those wounded men.

After being torpedoed on Dec. 7th, the *USS Helena* (at center) was moved to dry dock No. 2 for repairs. Lower right in dry dock No. 1 is the battleship *USS Pennsylvania* and destroyers *USS Cassin* (DD 372) and *USS Downs* (DD 375). US Navy photo taken on Dec. 19, 1942.

At a meeting of Peru Rotarians at the Hotel Peru on Mar. 19, Berghefer recounted how he was in the aft engine room of the *USS Helena* when a torpedo hit the ship. While assisting the wounded in getting off the ship, he was hit in the head by a falling overhead support. He ended up on the beach and spent the next four days in a Hawaiian hospital where he was treated for a skull fracture and concussion. He was finally given casualty leave and returned to see his parents, Mr. and Mrs. Adam Berghefer of 2415 Sixth St., Peru.

USS Helena U.S. Navy photograph dated 1940.

News of the war continued to filter in, bringing heartache to a number of families. One father especially hard hit by a Western Union telegram was Xavier Iwanicki of LaSalle. His two sons, Stanley, 22, and John, 19, were shipmates aboard the cruiser *USS Houston*.

USS Houston (CA-30). U.S. Navy photo. Circa 1930's.

Both young men had been home on furlough in the fall of 1940. According to the LaSalle *Daily Post*, their father received a telegram from the Navy Department only saying that the boys were "missing in action." Notifications never went into detail about the circumstances. The story of the engagement with the Japanese was not revealed until nine months later. The "Galloping Ghost of the Java Coast," as the ship was known, had been on patrol with the *HMAS Perth* and a number of other ships when it encountered the enemy fleet in the Battle of the Java Sea. After most of the Allied ships were sunk, the *USS Houston* and *HMAS Perth* continued to take on the Japanese fleet Banten Bay. The *Perth* was sunk, but the *Houston* continued the fight. According to official reports, it was hit by four torpedoes before it rolled over and sank. It was later confirmed that the Iwanicki brothers were killed in action in the Battle of Sunda Strait on Mar. 1, 1942.

Other Illinois Valley families also received the dreaded telegrams. On Mar. 16, it was reported that Clarence Shumaker, 22, and Joseph Dekeron, 21, both from Ottawa, were missing, but the newspaper had no details of what happened.

While these troubling stories were disseminated through the local news media, DePue continued to do its part on the home front by enlisting men in the armed forces as well as enlisting the services of civic organizations for a variety of support roles. Armed forces enlistments numbered 41. Notable among that number was Miss Myrtle Ellis, the only female to enlist. She served as a supervisor of nurses in Pennsylvania. Her brother, Jerry Ellis, joined as well. By the end of March, DePue residents had already oversubscribed to the Red Cross relief obligation with donations of over $1,400. The DePue Women's Club was sending "comfort kits" to the women of England and collected money to buy garden seeds for English Victory Gardens and an ambulance for the American military. The DePue American Legion and Auxiliary as well as the Boy Scout troop volunteered for any services asked for in home defense.

While the biggest contingents of inductees heading to Camp Grant, Great Lakes, and other training bases were coming from the larger cities in the Illinois Valley – 96 men left from the Tri-Cities in March – even the smallest towns sent their sons. Malden, for instance, had six men in the service by March 1942. Frequently, buddies would sign up together. On April 8, six young men from Jonesville and Piety Hill enlisted in the Marines. They included Clifford Hunter, John Rolando, Joseph Welch, Frank Gaull Jr., James Reynolds, and Joseph Hauptman.

In small towns especially, everyone was always anxious to hear about one of their local boys. Pvt. Don Seibert was able to write home to his parents in Utica about the conditions at his new station in Australia. He wrote that the mail was taking about a month to get "down under," and he said, the Aussies were "treating us as if we were their own soldiers."

To honor the young men joining the military, the Oglesby Women's Club resurrected the idea of having a service flag similar to the one they made in WWI. The design would be a white field with a band of red and blue stars bearing the names of the 150 serviceman who had been called to duty. Additional stars would be added as more men were called. Mrs. M.A. Moliske, club president, said she would appoint a service record chairman to keep a file of all the men in the service.

In mid-April 1942, the navy announced the establishment of the V-1 program for college freshmen and sophomores, who could enlist with the rank of apprentice seaman but continue their college studies. The navy encouraged the students to follow a curriculum which included math and physics. Men meeting the naval requirements would be qualified as naval reserve officers.

The issue that affected even more residents of the Illinois Valley was rationing. One of the first items to be on the rationed list was sugar. The government explained that Pacific fighting had caused a serious reduction in imports from Hawaii and the Philippines, which accounted for 27 percent of American sugar imports. The 35 percent of the sugar that came from the West Indies was curtailed by the scarcity of ships. Most of the available ships were now carrying vital war materials. The government explained that the uses of sugar went beyond canning and other home uses. It was also an important ingredient in the manufacturing of explosives.

In April, the Bureau County ration director, Burt Miller of Manlius, announced that 39,000 ration books would be issued in the county in May. It was estimated that it would require the services of one registrar for every 80 persons or about 500 workers to operate the rationing in Bureau County.

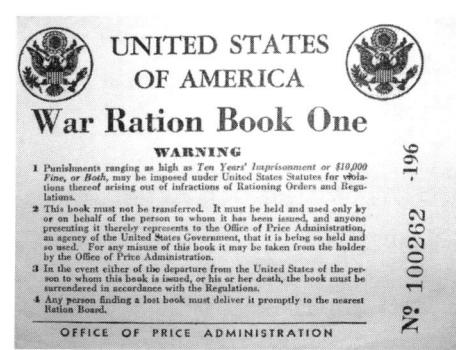

Application cards for a ration book were recommended to be on file for every man, woman, and child. While it wasn't mandatory to register, persons who did not have Ration Book One were warned that they would have considerable trouble in obtaining subsequent ration books. The public soon became aware of the seriousness of the situation when they went to their neighborhood grocery stores and found that no sugar was for sale, and none would be sold until the distribution of ration books had been completed.

On April 28-29, registration for sugar rationing began for tradesmen at Hall H.S. Wholesalers and retailers fell into separate categories and filed different forms. Civilians would register from May 4 to May 7. James Nesti, Superintendent of the Spring Valley Elementary School, was in charge of registration. Generally, teachers were recruited to serve as registrars.

When registering, the applicant had to provide a physical description of other family members to make sure that the holder of the book was the individual who had applied. In LaSalle, classes were dismissed on Monday and Tuesday while the faculty took down information from the parents of the children in the rooms as well as adults with no children in school. Others assisting with the registration process were special teachers, PTA volunteers, the American Legion Auxiliary, and the LaSalle Women's Club. Principal Matilda Harman of the Lincoln School and Principal Ella Boyle of the Grant School were in charge during registration.

Not everyone bothered to register. By May 6, about 4,400 individuals had registered in Spring Valley, but a final figure of 5,000 was predicted. When registration was completed on May 8, the number of applicants in LaSalle totaled 12,212, slightly less than the 12,500 expected.

In LaSalle County, 95,690 individual applications were recorded according to Arthur Jobst, chairman of the county rationing board. Over 2,200 individuals of that number were denied an application since they had too much sugar at home.

Homemakers in particular were concerned about how they were expected to can fruit and make jams and jellies with the limitations of rationing. Ed Kolowski, chairman of the LaSalle rationing board, assured them that they could apply for a special ration allotment of five pounds of sugar per person.

This War Ration Book dated May 5, 1942 for Clara Moyle of Oglesby indicates an allotment of 15 pounds of canning sugar. Oglesby Library.

Recycling was especially encouraged in every community. In April, the Peru Council of Defense asked that worn out suits, dresses and shirts be donated. Besides being used to clean war machinery, some of the material was turned into building material or reworked into other textiles. A new government regulation even outlawed cuffs on pants. Cut off material could not even be given to the purchaser of tailored pants.

There seemed to be a volunteer group forming for every imaginable reason. On May 6, 1942, an apprentice seaman from the Ninth Naval District spoke to a group of men at the South Shore Boat Club about the organization of an auxiliary unit of the Coast Guard Reserve in Peru. At the meeting, 20 boat owners expressed their desire to participate in the program to assist the Coast Guard during emergencies.

The daily news of fighting in the Pacific seemed insignificant compared to the news that a loved one was coming home. Mother's Day, 1942, was especially memorable for Mrs. John Klopcic, when her son, Anthony, came home unexpectedly. No one had heard from Tony since Dec. 26. He told his family that he had been serving aboard the light cruiser *USS Marblehead*, which came under attack by 54 Japanese planes near Balikpapan. The ship, launched in 1924, took two direct hits, which killed 17 and wounded 40. Klopcic was one of the lucky survivors.

Seaman Tony Klopcic of LaSalle fought in the Japanese air attack on Feb. 4, 1942 in the Java Sea. The *USS Marblehead* limped back to Tjilatjap, Java, for repairs to the bomb damage seen here next to its 6-inch gun at the stern. U.S. Navy photo.

The cost of the war continued to escalate, causing the government to seek more participation in war bond drives. The first factory in the Tri-Cities to display the coveted "Minute Man" flag was Illinois Zinc. In order to have that honor, the company had to enroll 95 percent of it employees in their biweekly payroll deduction plan. Westclox managers were frustrated in their early attempts to get employees to sign up. Although 74 percent of the workers did buy bonds, only 3.8 percent did so through the payroll deduction method.

On Monday, May 12, hundreds of "Minute Men" volunteers set out on a house-to-house campaign to sign up as many residents of the Tri-Cities as possible for additional savings bond pledges. The event began with a parade starting at L-P High School followed by speeches by Mayor Orr, J.E. Malone, chairman of the War Savings Bond and Stamp Drive in LaSalle, and M.J. Faletti, the LaSalle

City Attorney. At 6 p.m., a flyover and aerial show was scheduled by Vogel's Flying Service.

The children of Washington School were eager to do their part by buying war savings stamps at the post office every Wednesday. They set a goal of $1000, and exceeded it on May 14 with a total of $1055.75. Principal Paul Bone said that there would be an all school assembly as a culminating activity at the end of the month.

Every person who pledged to buy savings bonds and stamps was given this blue and white sticker for display in their windows.

The Tri-City draft board not only called on young men for duty but also, for the first time, signed up men who were overage, 45-65, in the fourth draft registration. While these older men were not expected to see military service, they were being called upon for their special skills. On April 27, about 3,300 men in this age category had signed up to serve. The first three men to be randomly selected were James Scalarini (LaSalle), Louis Caveletto (Oglesby), and Charles Amsler (Peru).

With so many local men heading off to Camp Grant and other posts, the local community was asked to participate in the "Bundles for America" Days in LaSalle-Peru. The basic idea was to supply each recruit with a kit full of personal articles such as shaving cream, toothpaste and brushes, soap, sewing kits, etc. It would only cost $1 to buy the needed supplies for each kit. Previously, residents of Ottawa had organized a similar effort hoping to collect enough money to furnish 100 kits. The citizens responded with enough money to outfit 1,000 kits! All of the kits were going to boys from the Illinois Valley.

Patriotism among Westclox workers grew with every passing month as more workers joined the military. The Staff and

Pinion Department decided to make an extra effort to display their patriotism. By collecting donations from the department employees, they purchased four American flags and placed them at various locations in their building. Funds over and above the cost of the flags were used to buy cartons of cigarettes to send to the men from the department who had enlisted in the armed forces.

Some of the Westclox women had completed a 12-week course in home nursing while still putting in long hours at the factory. The classes were taught on Tuesdays, Thursdays, and Saturdays by three registered nurses, Mrs. Mary Percival, Mrs. August Soedler, and Mrs. John Rock. On June 15, Miss Margaret McGreevy of the Hygienic Institute presented the 46 girls with certificates. Most of the girls were from LaSalle (28) and Peru (10). However, Spring Valley was represented by four of the students, and Oglesby and Ladd had two each.

Attention was now shifting to Seneca. On May 25, the LaSalle *Daily Post-Tribune* had reported that the Chicago Bridge and Iron Works won a government contract to build ships at its Seneca facility. The production of LST's on the banks of the Illinois River would require 1,500 welders alone.

One of the first steps in providing for the needs of workers coming to Seneca was housing. The photo shows one of the government housing complexes. Seneca shipyard would have 2,477 housing units of all types. *Our Prairie Shipyard.*

To handle the expanding workforce, the LaSalle County Housing Authority established a project called Seneca Defense Housing consisting of 675 family housing units and enough dormitories to house 350 single men on 45 acres. On June 16, another news report described the need for a further expansion so that 600 additional families could be accommodated on a 60 acre site just north of the Illinois River near Rt. 186. The early construction proceeded so quickly that housing was ready for 200 families within the week. In the meantime, new restaurants opened; vacant buildings were being used; the bakery business flourished; and trailers were parked in every available open space in town and on farmers' fields.

Another major economic development at the end of May was the formulation of plans for the construction of a Rock Island freight terminal with docks and offices adjoining the Ottawa freight house. Normally, only the larger cities had such facilities.

Meanwhile, news of those missing in action was released to the media in brief statements. Four local men were on the list in May: Cpl. Walter D. Batchelder, USMC (Peru), F2c Edgar C. Durfee (Ottawa), Cpl. Leroy Finch, USMC (Grand Ridge), and S1c Abe Jacobs Jr. (Ottawa). The War Department also announced that the Japanese held Pfc Alfred Pelligrini, USMC (Marseilles). He was captured at Wake Island and interned in Shanghai. He was one of the 20 POW's from Illinois at the time.

Reports of soldiers and sailors either returning home or out of harm's way always brought renewed hope and inspiration for the war effort at home. Pfc. George Gaede of Tonica managed to get back home for a ten-day furlough from duty at Camp Sutton, NC. A phone call from California by Sgt. William Malone brought joy to the Henry Malone family in Peru. William, who had not been home in two years, had seen action at Pearl Harbor and was able to call from Camp McDowell Angels' Island to let his parents know he was in training to become a pilot.

Hundreds of news items simply informed those at home of the status of their loved ones. For example, brief items in the *Post-Tribune* on June 3, reported that Pfc Joseph Migliorini of Mark was at Camp Forrest, TN, and S1c Elmer Pry of Mendota was serving on the *USS South Dakota* somewhere in the Atlantic.

The dangers of war sometimes came closer to home than anyone ever expected. Many men and women in the Illinois Valley found employment in various war-related industries. In some of these jobs, there was an inherent danger to the workers. On June 5, a banner headline in the LaSalle *Daily Post-Tribune* read, "Elwood Arsenal Explosion Kills 57." The explosion, which was felt within a 50-mile radius of the plant, destroyed one of the 12 buildings at the sprawling munitions complex that covered 15,000 acres. In spite of the destruction, dozens of injuries and loss of life, the other loading lines continued their work.

(Note- The Post Tribune revised the number of deaths to 51 the following day.)

A number of local residents had found employment at the munitions plant near Kankakee. Initial press reports indicated that Elwyn Sperber of Morris and Leo Ferrito of Spring Valley were killed, and Frank Strangfeld of Shippingsport (LaSalle) was missing. Others who were injured included Edward Alicki of Peru, who was working in another building six blocks from the explosion. Keith Chapman of Tonica and William Barnes of Ottawa worked at the plant but could not be located. The force of the explosion was so intense that many bodies could only be identified by fingerprints.

Sabotage was ruled out. A later investigation determined that a defective fuse had caused the explosion in the building, which was used to transfer artillery shells to freight cars.

Such deadly incidents were rare and were quickly overshadowed by delayed reports from battles overseas. A week later, the Navy Department finally released the news of the Battle of the Coral Sea in which the aircraft carrier *USS Lexington* was lost on May 8.

Over 2,000 men were on the *Lexington*, but because of the heroic efforts of the crew to extinguish the fires caused by a Japanese air attack, the navy estimated that over 90 percent of the crew was saved. The news had major significance for the mother of Boatswain's Mate first class Virdean Withrow. He was able to call his mother, who lived at 122 Bucklin, LaSalle, on June 14, and tell her that he was safe in San Diego. Withrow finally made it back to LaSalle for an 11-day furlough. At that time, he was able to reveal some of the details of the battle to Roger Noon, the

LaSalle *Post-Tribune* reporter. The ship was still afloat although it had been hit by four torpedoes and several bombs. He said, "Most of the men didn't realize the seriousness of the fire that was raging below decks. It was no use; the flames worked themselves below decks and spread almost from stem to stern. About 7:30 o'clock in the evening the order was given to abandon the ship."

USS Lexington was lost in the Battle of the Coral Sea on May 8, 1942.
US Navy photo.

Although Withrow was the only reported sailor from LaSalle on the *Lexington*, there were three crew members from Streator, Joseph Teyshak, Louis Wargo, and Edward Bradach. They survived and were later honored during Streator's 4th of July celebration. Another survivor was Seaman Watson Allan who wrote about his experience on the *Lexington* to Mr. and Mrs. Currie, his aunt and uncle, who lived at 1637 St. Vincent, LaSalle. He said that he was in the water for about 45 minutes after he had jumped overboard and was finally rescued by a passing destroyer.

Unfortunately, John Steel Jr., a Marine, who spent his youth in Oglesby, was reported missing by the War Department. The Steele family, which had moved to the Morris area, received the tragic news weeks after the engagement. It would not be until August that the family received a more detailed letter. The Navy Department later said that their son was one of 14 Marines killed in the attack on the *Lexington*. The commendation said, "They remained at their posts efficiently performing their duties during strafing, explosions of torpedoes in the near vicinity of the battery, and after an aerial bomb had exploded and fired a locker of heavy ammunition at the battery. They extinguished the fire; policed the battery; and readied the only remaining gun for further defense of the ship. As a result of their actions, they efficiently assisted in the defense of the *Lexington* by fast, accurate fire under extremely difficult circumstances." Posthumous commendations were sent out to the families of four other Illinois Marines as well.

Last known photo of the *USS Lexington* before it sank on May 8, 1942. Photos such as this were seldom released to the media for fear of the demoralizing effect they would have on the home front. US Navy photo.

Sympathy was expressed by neighbors, and news of these incidents inspired the home front civilians to be more willing to tolerate the inconveniences required by rationing. In the Streator area, the War Price and Rationing Board divided the job of sugar rationing into six deputy rationing boards at Ransom, East Wenona, Rutland, Tonica, Lostant, and Grand Ridge. Hours were established in each community so that families could begin planning for the canning season.

Sugar wasn't the only commodity that had to be conserved. In the summer of '42, there was a national effort to find as much rubber as possible so that gasoline rationing would not be needed. Local filling stations in the Tri-Cities volunteered to serve as depositories for the month of June. Everything made of rubber, from tires to garden hoses, baby dolls, and girdles, was accepted.

In Putnam County, the rationing board director, John Dore, gave notice of the hours of operation at the Highway Department Building in Hennepin to obtain applications for sugar canning permits. He also reiterated the admonition that if a ration book was lost, destroyed, or stolen, it would take at least two months before another book would be issued.

June 26 was the scheduled date for the start of a two-week scrap rubber drive. The Standard Oil Co. serving LaSalle County took charge of collecting everything from rain coats to suspenders, and galoshes – anything made of rubber the company spokesman said. Fifty collection trucks would drive to farms in LaSalle County, Spring Valley, and Granville. Standard Oil would pay a penny a pound for the scrap rubber and sell it back to the government. A company spokesman said, "No oil company will receive a penny of profit for this service." All of the money collected from the sale of the rubber was "pledged to the USO, Navy Relief, Army Relief, and the Red Cross." In Princeton, 40,000 pounds of rubber was collected at the railroad siding.

That same day marked the arrival of the Illinois War Production Caravan in LaSalle. Industrial production contracts from the federal government swamped some manufacturers, who needed to find subcontractors for much of the work. When the caravan arrived, two tractors, pulling trailer buses painted in "blueprint blue," parked across the street from the Kaskaskia Hotel. The units had been touring Illinois, Iowa, and Kentucky to display some of the 1,000 "bottleneck" parts badly needed by the military industries. It was hoped that after touring the exhibit, local manufactures would be interested in becoming subcontractors for the 70 prime contractors. During the one-day visit, about 30 men from 17 different factories in LaSalle County viewed the display.

Commonly seen in windows in WWII were service banners with red borders on a white field with a blue star for each member of the family or organization in the service. A gold star indicated that a serviceman had been killed. Streatorland Historical Society.

As more and more men were called to duty, it became popular for towns, factories, retail businesses, and even government offices to show their appreciation by displaying service banners. On July 8, 1942, John McCann, the postmaster in Oglesby, announced that he would put a service banner bearing three stars in his window. The stars were for former postal employees, Capt.

Joseph Meglich, Pvt. Clem Gillio, and Attilio Corredato, who had recently been drafted.

Celebrations were organized at every opportunity to raise the home front morale. Wednesday, July 1, was designated as "Retailers for Victory" Day to begin a major drive to sell war stamps and bonds. The effort started promptly at noon with the sounding of the fire and air raid sirens in Peru. Aerial bombs were launched from the lot north of Turn Hall. Their loud explosions resonated across the town. Charles Soedler also fired a miniature cannon on Fourth St. All sales in local retail stores were stopped for 15 minutes while clerks sold stamps and bonds. Volunteer women manned "Molly Pitcher" booths near business establishments to sell bonds and stamps. In LaSalle, a parade was led by the American Legion and the pumper from Fire Co. No. 1 followed by numerous floats and decorated cars. It was all part of a nationwide effort to promote the sale of defense bonds during July. Lawrence Meher, chairman of the retailers' organization was pleased with the initial sales.

"Remember Pearl Harbor" was chosen as one episode in the "American on Parade" historic pageant scheduled for July 3, 4, and 5 at Washington Park in Peru. The routine featured 24 ladies including Miss Victory and her Victory Belles as well as Miss Columbia. The "Red and Blue Air Girls" and the "Robot Girls" would represent the front lines and home front women.

These celebrations of community solidarity were backed up with constant efforts to find new ways for ordinary civilians to support the troops. Another solution to wartime shortages was explained by W.J. Aplington, commander of the LaSalle civilian defense council. It was pointed out that waste kitchen fats could be used to make glycerin which was the basis of dynamite and TNT. Margaret O'Brien, a former president of the American Legion Auxiliary, was appointed by Aplington to the position of chairman of the fats salvage committee. A similar effort was organized by Mrs. M.A. Moliske, chairman of the Oglesby Civilian Defense Committee. It was an important job since the war in the Pacific had cut off a major supply of vegetable oils. On July 29, Miss O'Brien released the names and locations of the butcher shops cooperating in the program in LaSalle. These included the

Ankiewicz Food Mart, Bartoli's, Bruder's, Buehler's, Cigolle's, Liberta's, Urbanowski's, Waszkowiak's, Zens, Mid-City Market, Brennan's, Brucki's, Chicago Butcher's, LaSalle Super-Market, Panneck's, Spitzmiller's, and Stachowiak's.

The salvage program was to be carried out, beginning with homemakers, who were encouraged to strain all waste fats and meat drippings and pour them into clean coffee or shortening cans. Once they had accumulated a pound or more, the cans would be taken to the local butcher who would pay 5¢ a pound. The butcher, in turn, would combine the contents of the cans with his own supply of waste fat and sell them to the renderer for 6¢ a pound. The government emphasized that the program would continue until the end of the war. The material was absolutely essential to produce the material needed to fill the bombs.

Defense bond sales continued to rise with each passing month. Surprisingly, McNabb led every town in the Putnam County in June, 1942 with $19,511. Granville and Hennepin contributed $5,418 and $3,925 respectively. Every town including Standard, Magnolia, and Putnam contributed several hundred dollars at a minimum. Overall, the county sold over $25,500 in bonds in one month.

Bonds sold even better in Marshall County with sales of almost $107,000. The effort was outstanding in Lacon which totaled over $27,000. Toluca came in with over $19,600; Wenona added $18,631; and Henry sold $15,160 in bonds. As in Putnam County, the smaller communities of Marshall County also made a significant effort: Varna - $14,362; Camp Grove - $7,775; LaRose - $2,262; Sparland - $1,362. These figures included the sales of a large quantity of Series G bonds, which could not be depended on every month. It was the continued pledges for the monthly Series E bonds that the government sought.

The government tried a variety of approaches to appropriate metal that was vitally needed for the construction of planes, ships, tanks and other weapons. Besides curtailing automobile production on Feb. 1, 1942, regulations were issued to halt the production of auto license plates on Mar. 18; curtail the production of razor blades on Mar. 31; ration bicycles beginning on April 2; and halt production of major appliances on May 31.

Even bicycles were being rationed. As of July 9, 1942, those individuals who needed bikes to ride to work would be able to obtain purchase certificates. From July 9 until Aug. 31, there was an allotment of 12,628 bicycles for all of Illinois. "Victory" models could be sold for no more than $32.50, a price fixed by the OPA. The *Spring Valley Gazette* reported that children's bikes were not being rationed. In July, only 14 certificates were being issued for bike purchases. Ed Kolowski, the chairman of the rationing board, said that in order to be eligible, an applicant "must travel quickly or frequently in delivering merchandise or messages." That translated into needing a bike at least three days a week in an occupation that contributed directly to the war effort, and, without a bike, the individual would have to walk at least three miles or spend at least 1½ hours in commuting. Those who could not obtain a certificate in July were told that they would have the first opportunity for available certificates in August.

OPA regulations affected the daily life of homemakers in many ways. Effective July 14, 1942, a letter grading system of "AA," "A," and "B" for beef and veal replaced the "prime," "choice," and "good" previously stamped on the carcasses. Ceiling prices were determined by the letter designation. OPA also encouraged homemakers to save their jars and lids. The reason, according to the *Spring Valley Gazette*, was "because jar covers, tin cans, bottles, and metal containers are marching off to war." That month, OPA announced some good news for homemakers. From July 10 until Aug. 22, ration stamps No. 5, 6, and 7 would allow for two extra pounds of sugar for each stamp.

Food rationing would have been even more restricted if it wasn't for the hard work at the nation's cannery workers. It was the sweet corn harvest season again, and that meant the J.B. Inderrieden Canning Co. in Mendota had to appeal for more workers to help in the "Food For Victory" program. Just about all of their workers were hired locally with the exception of a few specialists brought in from other Inderrieden factories in Wisconsin. For six weeks, the 1942 pack required the employment of mothers, daughters, grandmothers, and grandfathers since the young men were generally in the service or in war-related industries.

Housewives were also called upon to answer Gov. Greene's appeal to save kitchen grease and fat. Florence Denison, who served as chairman of the Mendota Fats Salvage Committee, announced that the ladies had turned in 2,000 pounds of waste fats. Of that amount, 12 percent could be turned into glycerin, which, when combined with nitric acid, produced nitroglycerin.

In mid-August, the state salvage committee sent out letters to local committees announcing that another scrap drive was needed. In response, R.C. Carter, the Mendota salvage committee chairman, appealed to farmers to look for broken down equipment; it would bring $8 a ton. Carter pointed out that all types of metal products were accepted including iron and brass bed frames, pipes, electrical cords, sash weights, electrical wiring, aluminum pots and pans, batteries, radiators, stove grates, lawn mowers, garden tools, etc. Scrap was collected at three locations in Mendota, the Alexander Lumber Co., the Gillette Produce Co. and the Farmers Co-Operative Elevator.

Salvage drives were a constant part of the civilian war effort. Certain metals were becoming so scarce that local problems developed. The National Sheet Metal Co. in Peru protested the confiscation of 40,000 pounds of copper sheets at its plant. The material had been sent to be chrome plated for a bathroom accessories company in New York. The War Production Board had other ideas. It offered the New York company 16¢ a pound for the commodity, which was valued at 66¢ a pound.

Even something as simple as a coat hanger became a salvage item. Maj. Howard Doan of Camp Grant appealed to Illinois Valley residents to bring as many wire coat hangers as possible to his home at 528 Fourth St. in LaSalle. He said he needed 4,000 coat hangers for the 1,200 men who were moving into tents at Camp Grant.

The government cut essential supplies of metals used in many local factories. So, it didn't really come as a shock when Westclox announced the termination of clock production effective July 31. The management hoped that war production work would fill the void, but until then, unemployment benefits would begin on Aug. 2 and last until Oct. 31 for those who were laid off.

Westclox workers watched as the last Big Ben came down the assembly line on July 31. The Peru plant had been turning out clocks and watches since 1885. The scarcity of metals caused a halt to production.
Tick Talk magazine, July 1942.

It took a great quantity of metal to produce the tanks, planes, and ships, so the government called for additional scrap metal drives. One collection effort had ended on July 9, but the War Production Board's Bureau of Industrial Conservation called for another drive to begin on July 13.

Joseph Riva served as chairman of the salvage committee in Spring Valley. According to the *Gazette's* Aug. 20, 1942 edition, "A good part of the heavy armament that goes into ships and tanks is made from scrap and it is necessary that this old metal keep flowing to the mills in an endless stream so that the program will not be held up."

The scrap drives continued into the fall. On Sept. 19, a special program titled "Get in the Scrap" was presented at the Spring Valley theater. There was free admission to the film "Across the Rockies," for anyone who would bring two pounds of scrap metal, rubber, rags, or other salvage material. Everything was loaded onto the truck of Solomon Barr, a member of the Spring Valley salvage committee.
A *Putnam County Record* ad announced another drive in August. Lawrence Thomas served as the chairman of the Putnam County salvage committee. Other members included Jesse Morris, Charles Read, Frank Ellena, Edward Loebach, Charles Johnston, and Henry Barr.

War bond sales were the order of the day on July 30 in the Red Room at the Hotel Kaskaskia. The LaSalle Retail Merchants promoted the bond sale that raised over $147,000. Seaman Eugene Radcliff of LaSalle, who served on the gun crew of a merchant ship that was sunk in the Atlantic, and Seaman Robert Healy from Chicago, who was decorated for bravery during the attack on the *USS Marblehead*, were among the honored guests. Ray Zarnicki accepted an "Emblem of Honor" on behalf of his mother, Caroline Zarnicki of Oglesby, who had five of her children serving in the armed forces.

Every aspect of wartime preparedness was constantly being stressed in community organizations. Although civil defense and blackouts were very real issues because of German U-boat attacks on the Atlantic Coast and the fear of a possible Japanese attack on the Pacific Coast, the War Department issued civil defense recommendations for the entire country.

Early in July, civil defense coordinators at every level were notified of a pending drill. The area participating in the blackout covered all of northern Illinois as well as four other states including industrial centers like Chicago, Gary, and Detroit.

W.J. Aplington, commander of the local civil defense council, together with Herbert Bekermeir, chairman of Peru's civil defense council, formulated the local plan. The warning would come with a five-minute, uninterrupted blast of whistles from factories throughout LaSalle and Peru. Factories could continue production, but exterior plant lights would be extinguished. The "all-clear" signal would be the relighting of all street lights. R.E. Davies, the civil defense coordinator for the area, called a meeting to discuss the test blackout for the Illinois Valley.

In Ottawa, chief warden Paul Devore said that three aerial bombs would be detonated to notify residents of the start of the exercise, and another bomb would be set off at the conclusion of the blackout. It was anticipated that an air raid siren would be used to signal future blackouts.

The alert date and time was eventually set for August 12 from 10:00 to 10:30 p.m. Numerous regulations were going to be enforced. Although police, fire, ambulance, and utility vehicles could be used during the blackout, all vehicle headlights had to be shielded. Sheriff Welter made sure that all of the police cars had their headlights properly shielded. All cars would also be required to park or pull off the road during the blackout. Illuminated signs would be turned off and store lights shielded. On the night of the blackout, village fire sirens were sounded in Putnam County at 9:57 p.m., church bells tolled in Spring Valley; factory whistles, the special air raid siren, and fire department siren sounded in Peru; and the whistles were blown at the Marquette and Lehigh cement plants in Oglesby to signal the beginning of the exercise. Auxiliary firemen and police officers were on duty at remote locations outside of Spring Valley. The American Legion had members guarding the bridge on Route 89. Members of the Civil Defense council guarded the pumping station and the telephone office. During the blackout in Ottawa, Sgt. Cyrus Bradish headed a squad of reservists from Company E of the Illinois Reserve Militia guarding the bridge over the Illinois River and the Marseilles locks. The Ottawa Boy Scout troop had volunteered for messenger duty.

As planners hoped, virtually every light was quickly extinguished in the cities and the country. Then, at exactly 10:30 p.m., the street lights came on, and there were "brief blasts from sirens and whistles," to signal the end of the exercise, according to the LaSalle *Post-Tribune*.

During the drill, Capt. Elmer Wolfe of Ottawa, a member of the Illinois Reserve Militia Air Corps, was an observer in a plane piloted by William Vogel, the owner of a local flying school. J. O. Oughton, another observer with Wolfe, reported, "The blackout was as perfect as could be expected under existing conditions." Certain lights were visible as they flew over LaSalle-Peru at an altitude of 2,500 feet. In addition to a few flickering lights in some of the rural farmhouses and the red and green traffic signals in LaSalle, Oughton said he could see lights at Westclox. In addition, the red glow from the open furnaces of the Matthiessen and Hegeler Zinc Company could be seen for a great distance.

The extensive planning had paid off with very positive results. Mayor Fred Spurgin, who served as the chairman of the Ottawa civil defense, was pleased with the cooperation of residents. There were a few problems in the commercial district. An electric clock light was still burning on Madison St. A few stores and even the court house had a couple of lights still on. On Brewery St. hill, one tavern was in violation of the regulations.

Officials in the Tri-Cities proclaimed that the drill was highly successful. One member of the defense council said, "It was indeed gratifying to find that the test could be carried out without any noticeable confusion or excitement and with so few violations. The few violations which were noted became more glaring because of the fact that the blackout approached almost completeness." Joe Caveletto, who was in charge of the drill in Oglesby, said that residents gave their fullest possible cooperation to the government. None of the numerous air raid wardens in Peru noted a single violation other than a few unofficial remarks about isolated "light-leakage"

Although the exercise seemed to be almost perfect, the LaSalle city council decided at their Sept. 8 meeting to ban activities that would compromise the total blackout regulations. A new ordinance banned loitering longer than five minutes; congregating in groups of more than five on public walkways; operating any vehicle other than for emergencies; lighting a cigarette outside; and allowing even the smallest glimmer of light to shine from a window. Violation of the ordinance could bring a fine of up to $200.

Only two violations were noted in Spring Valley. The owner of the Florence Beauty Shoppe went home without turning off the night light. The second violation was at the Dillon Drug Store on St. Paul St. where the sign light was left on. To comply with Civil Defense regulations, the electrical wires leading to the store were cut. Other than these two incidents, the Spring Valley blackout was also considered a success.

Bureau County villages and cities had virtually no violations. Mayor Floyd Avery praised the citizens for passing the first alert without a blemish. Al Henry, communications director, said that, in keeping with the phone regulations, there wasn't a single outgoing call attempted during the alert. Only a few lights could be seen from war plants and trains traveling between cities.

When the alert was sounded in Wenona, all car and bus traffic was stopped at the city limits. Mayor Harry Ellison and L.W. Parks and Edward Monser, co-chairmen of the Civil Defense Corps had planned well, and there were few problems.

The assessment of the blackout in the *Putnam County Record* was terse – "Putnam County Reporting: 100% blackout."

The story in Mendota was much the same. The only major exception to the total blackout involved the Conco factory, which was working on military orders for the government. Their lights were dimmed so they could continue production. The J.B. Inderrieden cannery shut off their machinery for the half hour test even though they were canning sweet corn. The processing of the sweet corn at the Mendota cannery had just begun on Tuesday, the day before the civil defense alert. Barricades were set up to prevent cars from traveling on the highways during the drill.

The successful blackout was credited to good planning by the Civilian Defense organization chaired by Mayor L.J. Oester; William Ashley was the local coordinator. The committee had even taken the precaution of raising the siren at the waterworks to the level of the surrounding buildings so that it could be heard at a greater distance. In addition, the managers of the Black Brothers plant agreed to sound their air whistle to alert Mendota residents to the start of the drill. The fire alarm system was disconnected, and all phone calls, except those of an emergency nature, were prohibited. All emergency communication had to be routed through one of the six district air raid wardens: Paul Stenger, Walt Elsesser, Roy McInturf, Forrest Fahler, Charles Salander, and James Ellis. Everything seemed to work as expected.

A successful air raid drill was just one of the ways in which the public cooperated to win the war on the home front. The federal government appealed to local newspapers to keep the information flowing about the need for more scrap and shortages of scrap for the furnaces of the steel mills. The *Spring Valley Gazette*, *Ladd Journal* and *DePue Leader* and other papers cooperated by running stories about the need for scrap metal. All sorts of examples were used to illustrate how unused items would help the war effort. For instance, one old flatiron could be turned into 30 hand grenades. A set of tire chains could be melted down for the metal needed in 20 anti-aircraft shells, and even a discarded kitchen sink contained enough iron for 25 3-inch artillery shells.

As the war went on, local servicemen were noted in Illinois Valley newspapers for their heroic conduct. One of those celebrated individuals was Lt. Oliver Doan from LaSalle. Doan's bomber crash-landed while attempting to rescue the crew of another bomber, which was forced down in the New Guinea jungles in May. Since neither plane could be repaired, Lt. Doan led the crews through the jungles living off the land until they were rescued. The news from Australia was not reported until late July.

Newspapers not only covered the battles overseas but also published numerous short stories of local men and women in the armed forces. A popular feature in the LaSalle *Post-Tribune* was its daily "Men in Service" column. It contained accounts of homecomings, promotions, casualties, and assignments. For example, on August 15, 1942, the paper reported that Pvt. Frank Mayzak of Oglesby was with an anti-aircraft battery in California; Pfc. C. Hawk, the son of Mrs. Maude Hawk of Ottawa, arrived in Australia; Drs. E.G. Barton and G.E. Gilman of Streator had been called to service; Louis Sever of LaSalle was promoted to Private First Class; Pvt Joe Schultz was on leave in Utica; and Pvt. Leon Heinz of Streator was missing in action in the Philippines.

Men who enlisted were often able to put their special qualifications to good use in one of the military branches. One of the St. Bede priests, Father Mark Rogan, OSB, felt that he could minister to the spiritual needs of the soldiers. He received notification in August that he was to be commissioned as an army chaplain.

The Knights of Columbus in LaSalle wanted to show their support for servicemen returning on furlough. A sign reading, "Welcome Servicemen – Your Uniform Is Your Pass" was hung over the main entrance of the club house. It was to be the first servicemen's center opened in the Tri-Cities. Everything – the reading room, pool tables, card tables, ping pong tables – was made available to any member of the armed forces.

Servicemen, who returned home on furlough, often told exciting stories never released by the War Department. Such was the case of Seaman Ed Podlinsek, who returned to a joyful reunion in August with his family at 545½ Todd St. in LaSalle. He had not been home in three years. During his brief visit, he told the press how his ship, the destroyer *USS Parrott*, engaged a Japanese convoy in a night attack in the Macassar Straits in January 1942. The Americans were outnumbered 10 to 1 but, according to Podlinsek, "We pulled a surprise on the Japs and got away with very little damage." After that, the *Parrott* fought in another battle at Bali. Two sailors were killed when the destroyer was hit by an 8-inch shell.

USS Parrott. US Navy photo.

Communities expressed unusual grief when it was announced that the first "local boy" had been killed. That was true when Princeton suffered the first of many casualties. A brief story in the *Bureau County Republican* told how Radioman 3c Hugh A. Middaugh died. He was on the transport *George Fox Elliot* in August 1942, when the ship was sunk by a Japanese dive bomber. Middaugh and other survivors swam to a deserted island that had neither food nor water. The Princeton sailor and some of the other crew sought relief by setting out in a launch, but it capsized in heavy seas. They took refuge in two rubber rafts, but on the ninth day, Middaugh died from exposure. A short time later, the rest of the men landed on another island and were saved.

Wenona also suffered its first casualty, F1c Francis King. He was killed on Nov. 30 during an attack on the *USS Minneapolis*.

In the fall of '42, stories of the Battle of Guadalcanal filtered home. In a letter to his father, Sgt. Bill Lohr of Tonica wrote about the action in the Solomons. "We have been a wee bit busy giving the Japs all the hell that you also said they deserved. I sure wish that I could tell you just what damage we have inflicted so far. I think that it would make you feel quite well for a while.

Of course, we have our bitter losses to take too, but I think that all the discomforts and hardships that are endured by the men here will some day be made up in some way."

One mother in Spring Valley was singled out for recognition of her sacrifice. In a special presentation in October 1942, Mayor Peter Ternetti presented the service mother's award to Mrs. Matthew Chorzempa of 224 E. Sixth St. She was the first mother in Spring Valley to have four sons in the armed forces. Members of the American Legion and VFW also took part in the ceremony held in the city council chambers.

On Oct. 18, Hennepin recognized its servicemen with a service flag dedication that began with a parade. The Granville American Legion color guard and Senachwine Township Band were followed by a number of floats. Miss Dona Morine, selected as the Dedication Queen, rode on the first unit. Hundreds of Putnam County residents followed the parade to the river bank to watch the dedication of a service flag on which 39 stars would be sewn for the 39 men in the service from Hennepin Township. Sen. Thomas Gunning from Princeton was the main speaker. Mrs. Viggo Cofoid was presented with the service flag, and Austin Allwood of the Hennepin Village Board was presented with an American flag. Part of the ceremonies also included reading the names inscribed on a bronze plaque of the 39 servicemen by Lyle Morine, a WWI veteran. Following the reading of a telegram from Pvt. Jack Brandstatter, his father, John Brandstatter Sr., made brief comments. At the conclusion of the ceremonies, Norma and Ray Marchiori were entrusted with the custody of the flags.

A Dept. of Information photograph of Lt. Albert W. Schinz, son of Mr. and Mrs. Fred Schinz of Ottawa and nephew of Mr. and Mrs. Tom Cawley of LaSalle, was printed in the *Post-Tribune* on Oct. 28. The 23-year old pursuit pilot had attended L-P-O Jr. College for two years and became a noted flier for having shot down a number of Jap Zeros while flying near New Guinea.

Huge quantities of food were needed to feed the men in the armed forces and help American allies. On Sept. 26, the Secretary of Agriculture announced that shipments of meat to the civilian market were going to be slashed beginning on Oct. 1. Although ration books were not going to be issued, as they were with sugar, the local butchers were going to have less meat to sell, at least for the remainder of the year. Quotas were based on the previous year's shipments. Beef and veal were set at 80 percent and pork was cut to 75 percent. The demand for lamb and mutton wasn't as great; 95 percent of those meats would be available for home front consumers. Secretary Wickard said that each individual would be allowed the equivalent of 2½ pounds of meat per week. Recalling the solution to food shortages in WWI, he suggested that restaurants "may prefer some such device as a meatless day."

News from the battlefields inspired others to do even more on the home front. The Tri-Cities Red Cross chapter sought additional volunteers to solicit materials for 400 comfort kits to be given to each serviceman leaving for foreign duty. The DAR, directed by Mrs. William Pouch in LaSalle County, had donated a mobile blood plasma unit and was trying to raise funds for additional equipment needed by the Red Cross. Even the management of the Aida Theater in Oglesby decided to take up the patriotic cause. Manager Anthony Potocnik announced that everyone who bought a bond at the bond rally at Washington school on September 1 would receive a free movie pass. Children who bought one 25¢ or two 10¢ stamps also received a pass for the Saturday matinee.

It marked the beginning of the month-long "Salute To Our Heroes" war bond drive. At 8:30 p.m., a parade from the school to the theater was led by a color guard unit from the Thomas Larkin American Legion Post. Carl Moellering (post commander), Valentine Aubel, Sam Politz, Art Mennem, and Joe Donatt carried rifles and flags at the head of the line of march. They were followed by the Oglesby school band under the direction of Everett Barrett.

Just to make sure that movie-goers wouldn't forget the real reason for their attendance, the film was interrupted so that

Harvey Dittle, a Minute Man, could give his pitch about war bonds. The effort was highly successful. Over $2,500 in bonds and stamps were sold. The biggest purchasers were employees of the Marquette Cement Co., who bought $1,500 in stamps and bonds.

The local schools always took an active part in the patriotic efforts. In the fall of 1942, the boys at L-P High School and L-P-O Junior College had some new elements added to their traditional gym classes. The school board had changed the curriculum to include close order drill and training in the manual of arms. Since actual rifles weren't readily available, the board authorized the expenditure of $22 to make 100 rifles. A new course, "Elements of Aeronautics," was also added to the curriculum. Only senior boys and girls could take the course. While it didn't teach the students how to fly, it gave them the basic classroom training for future certification as private pilots.

When the federal government called for the formation of a Victory Corps in every high school, L-P High School responded with a variety of new clubs organized as divisions within the corps. The yearbook staff devoted an entire section of the 1943 *Ell Ess Pee* to the Victory Corps activities.

The Victory Corps Council (pictured) included Bob Fowlie, Dick Waldorf, Bill Hall, John Huling (chairman), Dorothy Witalka, Helen Kaiser, Therese Kotecki, and Mary Parisotto.

The Aeronautics Division included; Betty Jean Thompson, Jo Anne Beaumont, Carl Carlson, Dorothy Witalka, Therese Kotecki, Don Anderson, Max Freudenberg, Bill McClary, Ted Jaskowiak, and Edmund Goodman.

The Model Airplane and Plane Spotting Club at L-P High School met in Mr. Christophe's wood shop and later in Mr. Rabe's room learning to build and identify Allied and Axis airplanes.

Mr. Petersen was in charge of L-P's military drill team in which both boys and girls were taught the manual of arms and how to march in formations. Since women were called to enlist in the WAACS, WAVES, and SPARS, it seemed appropriate to give the girls training as well.

The Radio Club learned many valuable skills for future members of the armed forces. Mr. Lefler taught pre-flight aeronautics and also directed the International Code Club that met every day at 7:45 a.m. to learn to decipher the dots and dashes of Morse code.

The War Map Club kept everyone informed about the progress of the war throughout the world. Other L-P students volunteered as fire and air raid wardens or joined the Camouflage Club.

Francis Harmeski and Bob Janko put up a poster made in the L-P art class to promote war bond sales.

War Stamp brokers in each homeroom tried to get 90 percent of the students to buy stamps so that they could buy a Minute Man flag for the school.

Photos-Ell Ess Pee 1943 Yearbook.

Ottawa H.S. also had students involved in clubs and activities to support the war effort. The Wireless Club was organized so students could learn about the operation of radios and to send and receive Morse code. The call for a Victory Corps in every high school resulted in the formation of an OHS club that promoted victory gardens and helped local farmers find students who would be willing to work for local farmers.

Mr. Glenn Scott met with the Victory Corps at Ottawa H.S. in Room 306 after school on Wednesdays in 1942-43. Ottawa yearbook, 1943.

Some organizations had to be restructured at Ottawa H.S. The interest in the military suffered a setback for the Officers Club. Gas rationing forced many of the boys, who were interested in being part of the military organization, to drop out. In addition, Mr. Shannon, who was the advisor, did not have the time to devote to the young men since he had additional duties with the State Militia. Since there was no club, the traditional military ball had to be cancelled. The Officer Cadet Corps renewed the traditional ties with the military the following year.

Streator H.S. students and teachers also assisted in registering citizens for ration books and bond drives. In the home economics department, 120 girls helped the Red Cross with sewing and knitting projects. The Out-of-School Youth Admin. held evening courses for boys and girls in the machine shop. Other evening classes were sponsored by the Flink Implement Co. to train area farmers in tractor, truck, and car repair. The local civil defense council also held its meetings at the high school.

It wasn't just high schools that offered young people an opportunity to get involved. Oglesby School Superintendent, J. Richard Evans reported in September 1942 that the teachers and students collected over $2,200 in bonds and stamps from January to May 1942. The children quickly got into the stamp buying habit, purchasing greater amounts every month. In October alone, the children purchased almost $600 worth of defense stamps. It was a major increase over the $100 per week usually sold.

The navy was always looking for recruits for their aviation program. They enlisted the support of the LaSalle Chamber of Commerce, which sent out 1,000 invitations to recent graduates from L-P, Hall, Earlville, Mendota, Princeton, Granville, Tonica, and Lostant high schools to try their skills at handling a flight trainer. LaSalle newspaper ads called for graduates between the ages of 18 and 26 to come to the corner of First and Gooding Streets on Sept. 16 to see if they could fly it. Ads promised an ensign's commission in the navy or a second lieutenancy in the Marine air corps as well as $245 a month to those who successfully completed the training.

The US Army didn't want to be overlooked in the search for recruits and the sale of war bonds so, on Sept. 18, an army jeep was brought to LaSalle from Bloomington. For one day, it was located in front of the LaSalle National Bank. The following afternoon, it was moved to the Peru Theater. Those who bought bonds were offered a free ride.

While much of the news regarding scrap drives focused on the cities and towns in the Illinois Valley, various farm-related companies, such as Ottawa Implement, Wallace Grain and Supply in Ottawa, Flink Implement in Streator, Linne Brothers of Troy Grove, the McCormick Deering Store in Tonica, L.J. Oester in Mendota, the Lostant Grain Co. and Snyder Implement in Wenona, to name a few, sponsored a scrap drive in the rural areas.

A total of almost 2.2 million pounds of scrap iron and steel and almost 80,000 pounds of scrap rubber were collected from the farmers in LaSalle County from Jan. 1 to Sept. 16. Farmers in Dimmick Township led the way with almost 300,000 pounds of iron and steel. The largest collection of scrap rubber –

over 7,000 pounds – came from Grand Ridge.

Next, came a salvage drive sponsored by the nation's newspapers. Beginning on Sept. 28, the vacant lot at Second and Wright Streets in LaSalle was used to drop off scrap metal and rubber during the three-week effort. Students at LaSalle public schools were organized into a Junior Army to collect scrap. The superintendent was "Colonel" E.G. Miller. Principals were "majors," and every teacher was a "captain." Each class would be an army company. Outstanding students were organized into Junior Rangers, Junior Commandos, and, for the girls, Junior WAACS. According to the *Post-Tribune* on Sept. 30, the student slogan would be "We are ready – ready for war – ready for victory – ready for peace." The watchwords were "Save, Serve, Conserve." The newspaper had stickers (at right) printed with red letters to be given to every household that contributed scrap.

Besides promoting the scrap drive, the LaSalle *Post-Tribune* had already shown its dedication for the war effort by printing a massive 120-page Victory Edition on March 21, 1942. It included almost 900 photos of servicemen from the area, each of whom received a copy of the special edition. The paper also proudly hung its service banner with three stars to honor former employees, Cpl. Francis Arnold (LaSalle), Pfc. Clayton Dowell (Peru), and Pfc. Donald Dickinson (LaSalle).

As an incentive to go "all out" on Oct. 9, "Buddy" Ebsen and "Skeets" Gallagher of Hollywood fame were on hand for a scrap rally at the LaSalle Theater in the morning. After a lunch at the Kaskaskia, they were taken to another rally at the Peru Theater. Only kids under 16 were allowed to enter the theaters to meet the comedians and see the movies free of charge. No one over 16 was allowed inside the theater even if they wanted to pay for a ticket. The show was strictly for the younger crowd.

In keeping with the patriotic fever, and not to be outdone by LaSalle-Peru H.S., the students at Hall H.S. under the direction of Supt. Allen Tyler went house to house on Friday and Saturday, Oct. 9-10, to pick up scrap. The Spring Valley grade school kids also pitched in. In return for their services, each student was promised the value of the scrap collected in war savings stamps. Service baskets were placed on every corner in Spring Valley, and another container was located at the Spring Valley Theater. Raymond Stutz was in charge of the student effort at DePue and Charles Fiocchi was responsible for the students in Ladd.

The results of the student collections were published in the *Spring Valley Gazette* on Oct. 22, 1942. The amounts collected exceeded all expectations. A total of 109 tons of material were collected. In Spring Valley alone there were "78 tons of iron, 1200 pounds of rags, 800 pounds of rubber, 1000 pounds of copper, and 150 pounds of other metals." One of the largest single contributors in Spring Valley was Western Sand and Gravel Co., which added eight tons of scrap. It was sold to dealers for $85. Even the old WWI cannon in the city park was added to the scrap pile.

Like Spring Valley, Ladd authorities decided to remove the mounted cannon in their city park and add it to the scrap collection. In addition, the Ladd children collected 20 tons of scrap, which included 420 pounds of old tires, a half ton of rags, 600 pounds of copper and brass, and 100 pounds of other metals.

Everyone was involved. The school children in DePue collected 15 tons of scrap, while the Seatonville kids collected 2,500 pounds. Dalzell added another 3,000 pounds. The Spring Valley paper pointed out that Mineral Point Zinc Co. had sold 1,400 pounds of metal and was shipping metal scrap every week.

The final total in LaSalle alone was upwards of 450 tons. Two major industries, Matthiessen & Hegeler Zinc Co. and Alpha Cement, were credited with donating 110 tons of scrap.

Oglesby collected 100 tons of metal thanks to the efforts of two WPA employees who went house to house, canvassing the entire city. Smaller towns contributed less, but every pound helped. Tonica had a total of 25 tons; Wenona had 50 tons, slightly better than the 48 tons found in Utica by children scrounging up 8 tons alone on one day. Rutland and Tonica each totaled 10 tons.

One of Peru's major industries, the Star Union Products Co., donated 10 tons of obsolete machinery to the scrap metal drive and announced that it was starting to bottle its beers in quart bottles to save the metal from the bottle caps. Star Union Products was also going to be the officially designated collection agency for tin cans.

This Victory Quart ad pointed out that the new quart-sized bottles would save metal on bottle caps, and it was more economical to buy quarts rather than the smaller 12 oz. bottles. LaSalle *Post-Tribune*, Oct. 10, 1942.

In Putnam County, Henry Barr was responsible for collecting the metal and rubber in Hennepin and Granville Townships. Local director Lawrence Thomas reported that he had received a telegram from the state saying that the scrap amount collected qualified the county for the Salvage Merit Banner from the WPB. The $201 collected from the scrap drive was donated to the American Red Cross and the USO.

Seventy counties in Illinois had exceeded the quotas set by the state in the August 1- October 31 scrap drive. In recognition of that effort, plaques were awarded to each of the counties including, Bureau, Marshall, Putnam, Lee, and LaSalle Counties.

In addition to the plaques, J. C. McDougall, assistant executive secretary to the Illinois WPB, presented Edward McMahon, the scrap salvage chairman of LaSalle County, a pennant (at left) to fly over the Ottawa court house in recognition that the county went over the top in the collection of scrap iron. The county ranked fifth highest in counties of 100,000 and more in population outside of Cook County. A quota of 100 pounds per person was set, and the per capita total collected in LaSalle County was 157 pounds.

There was a persistent fear that the major steel mills were running out of scrap, but the newspaper-sponsored project turned the tide. L.J. Rosenwald, conservation chief of the War Production Board, told the newspapers, "There is no evidence now of any steel mills closing down." However, he predicted that scrap shortages would be a "continuing problem and will be with us as long as we are at war."

The Ottawa High School Marching Band and drill team took part in a parade to highlight one of the scrap metal drives. Ottawa 1943 Yearbook.

The Wenona Service Club, started on Oct. 9, 1942 under the leadership of Nell Pickard, also joined in the scrap metal drive. The Wenona school band paraded down Main St., where people gathered to hear speeches and sing patriotic songs.

Just as important as the scrap metal drives was the effort to collect old tires. In November 1942, there was a nationwide effort to collect as many tires as possible. The collection point in Spring Valley was the Railway Express Office. The paper reported that the week-long effort paid off with over 500 tires being deposited. Part of the reason behind the high turnout was a new regulation that said that no car owner could have more than five tires.

One of the only problems that developed was the lack of triplicate government forms that had to be filled out for each tire. Motorists were given the choice of donating the tires outright or accepting war stamps or a government check.

News of more potential shortages came from the Office of War Information (OWI) on Nov. 9. This time, the government worried that natural gas would be in short supply unless conservation was adopted by the citizens. A pipeline from Texas was the source for natural gas going to Spring Valley, Peru, and Oglesby. LaSalle manufactured its own gas. The WPB was going to limit reserves held by all distribution companies north of Shelbyville. Without cutbacks on the part of consumers, the OWI said that there would be acute shortages.

A new recycling effort began in mid-November to collect discarded silk, rayon, or nylon hose. Silk hosiery was needed in the manufacture of gun powder bags, which burned completely when a shell was fired. The other types of nylons were needed for other war materials. Margaret O'Brien, who had been in charge of organizing the collection of cooking fats, assumed the duties of the new project for LaSalle. In Oglesby, Mrs. Moliske took charge. Collection containers were set up at the Reizner Store, Personality Frock Shoppe, and Ferrari's Mode Shop. As soon as 100-300 pounds of nylons were collected, they would be packed up and sent by J. Reizner to the New York headquarters.

A few weeks later, the Secretary of Commerce, Walter Wagner, issued a bulletin saying that gasoline would have to be rationed. With the looming prospect of gas rationing in a few weeks, Oglesby mayor Frank Moyle appointed James Gallo as administrator for a program called "Share Your Rides."

Motorists in the Illinois Valley would register for a gas ration book on Nov. 9, and rationing was scheduled to begin on Nov. 22. Application blanks were made available at service stations, the *Post-Tribune* and local schools. Children were encouraged to take the blanks home to their parents to be filled out to speed the registration process. Teachers and members of the PTA volunteered to serve as registrars.

There were simple forms to fill out to get the standard "A" book that would allow a person to purchase up to four gallons a week. With the typical 1930's car, that would be enough to drive 2,880 miles a year! The "A" books contained four pages of eight coupons each. They expired after two months.

Of course, there were ways to get more gas. There were also "B" books with 16 coupons with various expiration dates for those who needed to commute more than 150 miles per month to get to work. Defense plant workers could apply for the eight-page "C" book with eight coupons for four gallons each, which was issued in addition to the "A" book. Those who got around on a motorcycle were issued "D" books. Truckers and taxi cab owners were issued "T" books. The government even considered off-highway vehicles and motor boats for which "E" and "R" books were available. Congressmen were in a special category. If they claimed that almost all of their mileage was "for official business," they could claim an "X" book for unlimited gasoline consumption. Farmers were also allotted all the gas they needed.

On the other hand, local municipalities faced shortages for their police and fire departments. Initially, Peru was given an allotment of 9 gallons for the fire truck in December and 25 gallons for the following three months. The Peru police car was allotted 500 gallons per month. The hardest hit of the municipal services was the Peru's street department, which operated two trucks, but these were compelled to operate with total of 55 gallons for all of December. The prospect of snow-packed streets in the coming months caused Mayor Al Hasse to seek additional gas. No notice had been received for the other trucks in the water and light departments. In addition, the new regulations specified that the tires on all vehicles would have to be inspected every 60 days at the owner's expense.

Teachers and students were recruited to help with the registration process. Hall H.S. faculty members, Harrison Tonev, Richard Nesti, and Dominic Marchiando, supervised the Hall seniors as they assisted motorists in filling out the paperwork. Only about 600 residents were able to complete the applications because the Princeton board failed to send enough forms. The process continued for a second day so that everyone could register.

With the prospect of limited gas availability, motorists nationwide lined up at the pumps prior to the first day of gas rationing. Locally, tanker trucks were pulling into filling stations 3-4 times on Nov. 30. As might be expected, Dec. 1, the first day of rationing, was a slow day at the pumps. One Spring Valley station had sold 3,000 gallons on Monday but only 35 gallons on Tuesday. Service stations still had some business. A cold front with zero-degree temperatures that swept across the Midwest spurred additional business in the sale of antifreeze.

Another shock came on the morning of Nov. 22 when all coffee sales stopped. Grocers had one week to restock their shelves so that they were ready for rationing which would officially begin on Nov. 29. Everyone over the age of 15 would be allotted one pound every five weeks – enough for about one cup of coffee every day. Rather than issuing new ration books, the WPB said to use the last coupon in the sugar ration book to buy coffee.

Some people questioned why coffee was being rationed since there was plenty of coffee available in Brazil. However, since there was only a 2-3 month supply in the US at any one time, and people were beginning to hoard coffee, the government felt rationing was the fairest way to distribute the limited supplies.

The entire program of rationing, whether food, tires, or gas resulted in a complicated, and sometimes frustrating system to make sure that ration coupons were redeemed before their expiration dates. The burden was shared by the consumer as well as the retailer. For instance, gas station attendants had to make sure that a motorist had sufficient unexpired coupons for his purchase. By mid-December 1942, only coupon No. 3 could be used until Jan. 31, 1943. Officially, the information in each book had to be checked to make sure that it corresponded with the number of the car's license plate. The correct number of coupons had to be removed from the book by the dealer before gas was dispensed into the car's gas tank; no spare tanks could be filled.

The government cautioned dealers who would be tempted to sell only to their favorite customers or to sell in violation of any other OPA regulation. Spot checks would be made by state OPA investigators to make sure that the gasoline being sold matched the numbers of coupons colleted. When the whole process started on Dec. 1, dealers were only given inventory coupons for their maximum storage capacity.

The ration book application deadline for sugar and coffee was set for Dec. 15. It was essential to have Ration Book One in order to receive Ration Book Two after Jan. 1, 1943.

Shortages caused by war in the Pacific also generated needs for products other than rubber and sugar. Because of a shortage of rope fibers normally imported from Manila and other areas of the Pacific, the government promoted a plan to grow hemp in certain areas, which included northern Illinois. The area was selected because of the favorable soil type. Processing plants would be constructed to process the cut hemp brought in from 4,000 acres in the immediate vicinity. Farmers, who wanted to grow hemp, had to live within 15 miles of the plants. The government would supply all the necessary cutting and harvesting equipment needed for this specialized crop. It was estimated that hemp harvests would generate about $120 per acre and, after deducting costs, the average producer was expected to realize a profit of $70 per acre.

On Dec. 10, 1942, the *Spring Valley Gazette* reported the government planned to build hemp processing plants in Ladd, Earlville, Minonk, Wyoming, Sandwich, and 11 other towns in northern Illinois. Each facility would employ about 100 workers, one-third of which would be women. Henry, Bureau, LaSalle, Putnam, and Marshall Counties made up part of the 17-county growing area. The plant in Ladd would cost about $350,000 for the building and machinery to process the hemp. The funds would come from the Commodity Credit Corporation. The following year would result in the legalized harvesting of the hemp stalks. Nobody seemed to care much about any uses for the hemp leaves (a.k.a. marijuana).

The anniversary of the bombing of Pearl Harbor did not go unnoticed. The theme of the day reflected at theaters was "Avenge Dec. 7th." William Harding, head of the local war theater committee, paid tribute to the moviegoers in LaSalle-Peru in recognition of their bond purchases through the theaters.

On Dec. 8, the Peru American Legion announced a "jalopy drive." Legionnaires would search the local area to find abandoned cars that had not been taken to a junk yard. They were also on the lookout for any type of heavy metal to assist the salvage committee of the Peru Civil Defense Council.

At the Dec. 11 Peru city council meeting, Mayor Hasse said that a local sign painter, Otto Karlosky, had suggested that an honor roll of the more than 500 Peru servicemen might be painted on the north side of the Welland Building on the southeast corner of Fourth and Peoria Streets, replacing the city's electric stove sign. Hasse said, "As long as we are not allowed to sell stoves, it might be as well to have the honor roll if it does not cost too much money." After a short discussion, a motion by Alderman John Wardynski to proceed with the project was adopted.

For months, activity at the Seneca shipyard had been carried on at a feverish pace. Sections of LST's (Landing Ship, Tank) had been welded together as quickly as possible. Crowds flocked to Seneca on Sunday, Dec. 13, for the launching of the first LST on the Illinois River. It had only taken six months for the pasture to become a fully functional shipyard. The honor of christening the first ship went to Mrs. Harriet Williamson, one of the few female welders at the shipyard. The Minooka woman had lost her husband in the Elwood munitions explosion. Before an estimated crowd of 7,000, Mrs. Williamson smashed a bottle of champagne against the hull. Seconds later, the ship slid sideways into the river where final outfitting would be completed.

Frank Bazzoni, the official shipyard photographer, kept a daily log of the launchings and other significant events at Seneca. On Dec. 13, he wrote, "First Ship Launched – A thrill if ever there was one. The weather was extremely cold, a few degrees above zero." Frank Bazzoni's identification badge. Seneca library.

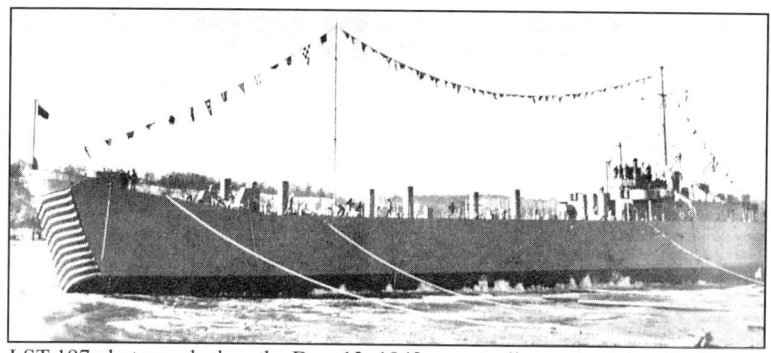

LST 197 photographed on the Dec. 13, 1942, eventually received four battle stars for participation in the occupation of Sicily, and the landings at Salerno, Anzio, and Normandy. Harry Volant of Ladd, who was one of the soldiers in the Anzio invasion on Feb. 21, 1944, also helped in the construction of this ship.
Our Prairie Shipyard 1942-45.

Undoubtedly, the activity at the Seneca shipyard produced the most indelible memories for the thousands of Illinois Valley residents who worked on them and saw the numerous launchings into the Illinois River. However, beginning in December 1942, there were other occasions when one might have actually seen not only LST's but also submarines floating down river.

The navy decided to build dozens of submarines at an inland port in Wisconsin. A contract was signed with the Manitowoc Shipbuilding Co., and construction of the first ship started on June 18, 1941. The first ten boats were designated as Gato Class. The government later placed an order for 20 more subs, 4 Gato Class and 16 Balao class.

The first sub, the *USS Peto* (SS-265), was launched into the Manitowoc River on April 30, 1942. After undergoing sea trials in Lake Michigan in the winter of 1942, the periscopes, along with the radar and antenna masts, were removed. The boat was loaded onto a specially built dry dock, measuring 330'x 64' with a draft of 7'. That was shallow enough to navigate the Illinois and Mississippi Rivers to New Orleans. The dry dock was located at the butterfly dam near Lockport. Once the sub was loaded into the dry dock, the tow was moved to the Illinois River. It was held up at Morris during the last week of December because of high water, but was able to move down river in January 1943.

USS Peto is pictured with periscopes and radar and antenna masts removed in a dry dock being pushed by the towboat *Kansas City*. About once a month, from 1943 until 1945, residents of the Illinois Valley could see submarines being moved in floating dry docks down the Illinois River to the Mississippi River destined for New Orleans

Many factories in the Illinois Valley didn't make quite the splash as was seen at the Seneca shipyard, but employees in war production plants in the Valley did whatever they could to support the troops. There was little that could be said about the materials being made. It was all classified. However, there were patriotic projects sponsored by the companies that could be described in the local newspapers.

In Oglesby, a parade was held on Dec. 19 to highlight the efforts of the Eicor workers. Marchers included the L-P High School band, six army MP's, a color guard from the American Legion post, and cars carrying dignitaries to the plant. After the American flag was hoisted, a Minute Man flag was also raised at the plant in recognition of the workers 100 percent participation in payroll deduction for defense bonds.

This LaSalle *Post-Tribune* cartoon on Dec. 18, 1942 illustrated the monetary contribution of Oglesby's Eicor factory to pay for an army jeep.

Henry Sauer, vice president in charge of production at Eicor, presented Army Capt. Stanton Prentiss with a check for $931 to cover the approximate cost of a jeep. This was the second time Eicor had donated money to buy a jeep; the Chicago plant had made a similar contribution in November.

Before the end of the year, there were more stories related to the men and women in the armed forces. The LaSalle newspaper pointed out that hundreds of men had been drafted for service, but the women were all volunteers. In Spring Valley, Delores Phillips, the daughter of Mr. and Mrs. Henry Phillips, was the first women to volunteer for the WAACS from her town. Betty Sczepaniak, daughter of Mr. and Mrs. Jacob Sczepaniak, had the similar distinction in Peru. The first WAACS from Oglesby were Mary Kernz and Caroline Kernz.

Visits from servicemen were also noted. Seaman John Engel, surprised his parents, Mr. and Mrs. Albert Ristau in Peru in December. The former L-P basketball star had survived the sinking of the *USS Leedstown* when it was torpedoed on Nov. 9 by the U-331 near Cape Matifou, Algiers during landings in North Africa. Another young man, who saw fierce fighting, was Marine Sgt. Edward Fristock of Oglesby. He was only able to tell the story of the fighting on Guadalcanal through an AP news release. In the report he said, "We knocked off about 20 Japs. I was hit just above the eye by a fragment of a hand grenade." After the fire fight, he was promoted to platoon sergeant.

Sgt. Fristock of Oglesby described how the Guadalcanal fighting resulted in heavy losses on both sides. Pictured is the beached Japanese ship *Kinugawa Maru*.

US Navy photo.

Workers at the Anthony Co. in Streator could see in their company magazine, *Shop News*, how the bomb carriers they built were being put to good use on Guadalcanal after Henderson Field was captured. Streatorland Hist. Society.

As the first full year of WWII came to an end, the last of the bonds sales were tabulated in Marshall and Putnam County in December. Wenona's total of $20,925 was the highest amount from any town in Marshall County. Toluca had the second highest sales with $17,437. McNabb still led the way in Putnam County with a grand total of over $12,000 of the $31,875 in the county. Both counties exceeded their goals. But for 1943, the goals were ratcheted upward again.

The year ended on a positive note with the announcement by D.H. Goodwillie, executive vice president of Libbey-Owens-Ford, that military contracts would soon result in increased hiring. Goodwillie said, "It has taken months not only in finding ways and means to do special jobs, but in lining up types of war work we could handle. We are now entering into actual production. I would like to explain the type of airplane sub-assemblies we are beginning to make in Ottawa and the production program on which we will soon be engaged, but these are 'military secrets'. Aircraft cabin and windshield assemblies are now being fabricated and shipped to companies producing this country's pursuit planes, scout bombers, and other planes for our armed forces." Eventually, it was learned that those orders would include windshields for F4U Navy Corsairs, P-47 Thunderbolt's, and canopies and nose assemblies for B-29 Super Fortresses. All of the Ottawa plant was involved in different aspects of producing the war materials, and Goodwillie predicted that the payroll would be greatly increased as volume increased.

In Lee County, another major war contractor, the Green River Ordinance Plant (GROP) near Amboy was just beginning to reach full production. In March, the federal government completed the purchase of over 8,000 acres of farm land and moved over 50 farm families. Construction began on April 11, but the plant was not ready to start manufacturing until October. A 25-mile complex of rails had to be laid out to tie into the Illinois Central and Burlington Railroad lines, one of the key factors in locating the plant a few miles outside of Amboy. The 24/7 construction phase required an estimated 12,000 workers who filled empty rooms in the Dixon – Sterling – Rock Falls area. Many GROP production buildings were interconnected but spaced far enough apart to meet the safety concerns related to explosive materials.

Under construction is one of the dozens of GROP "igloos" that would be used to store munitions. (Paulsen collection).

The first munitions line was ready for loading by the end of October. At first, the plant started turning out fuses and rifle grenades. In November, another line was set up to produce 75 mm armor-piercing projectiles used by Sherman tanks. The 155mm projectiles started coming off the line on Dec. 8. By the middle of December, Line 3 was opened for the 1600-pound bombs.

Exterior and interior photos of a finished "igloo" at GROP. The concrete "igloos" were covered with earth and separated from each other for safety reasons. (Paulsen collection).

Workers filled some munitions with black powder which came from the Badger Ordnance Plant in Baraboo, WI. High explosive shells were filled with a yellowish liquid called tetryl, which was more explosive than TNT. The liquid was mixed in large vats (right) in the plant and poured into the shells. Other ingredients included pentolite and cordite.

(Note-Because of wartime security, the actual production information remained classified until the end of the war.)

By the end of December, over 2,000 men and 1,000 women were working for the Stewart-Warner company. But those numbers would change substantially in 1943. Many of the employees came from Dixon, but others traveled much farther coming by bus because of gas rationing. The Oglesby Motor Transport and Peoria-Rockford bus lines brought workers from LaSalle-Peru-Oglesby. Those living in Spring Valley, Ladd, and Cherry usually took the Oglesby bus. The Rodney Brown Bus Co. and Dixon Transit ran buses to Princeton. Car pooling was essential for those wishing to drive their own cars.

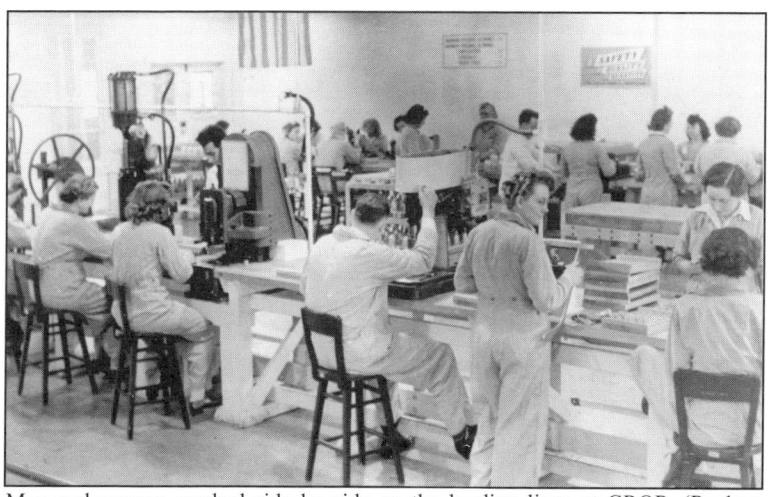

Men and women worked side by side on the loading lines at GROP. (Paulsen collection).

Workers, young and old, came from many local towns. Helen Scott (LaSalle), Helen Martin (Spring Valley), and Clara Harris (Princeton) were just three of the inspectors at the plant. Maude Peterson (Walnut), age 66, and Clara Reynolds (Oglesby) age 68, were among the oldest employees at GROP.

The huge facility with 420 buildings required hundreds of security guards. Cpl. J. C. Manning and Henry Orr came from Mendota, and Cpl. J. W. Chase drove to Amboy from LaSalle. When the plant first opened, horses were used to patrol, but in July 1943 they were replaced with motorcycles and cars. Duane Paulson, *Memories of the Green River Ordinance Plant 1942-45,* pp. 10-18.

Dr. Gerald S. McShane from Spring Valley took the position of medical director at GROP. His son, John McShane, was one of the construction workers at the plant. As an apprentice seaman in the V-1 program, John continued his education in pre-med at Milwaukee University.

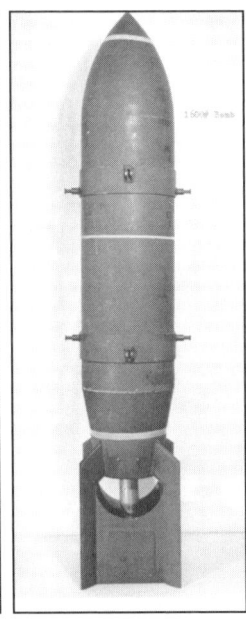

Far left: A 155 mm projectile (without fuse and explosives) of the type manufactured at the Green River Ordnance Plant. Projectile located at the Pankhurst Memorial Library in Amboy.

Left: a 1600-pound bomb assembled at GROP.
Paulsen collection.

Other GROP ordnance included from left to right: M6A1 rockets, M9A1 rifle grenades, 105mm and 75 mm projectiles. Paulsen collection.

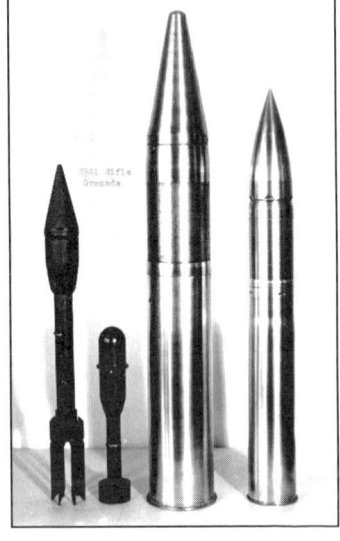

CHAPTER THREE
Another Year of Sacrifice

The spectacle of a submarine being moved down the Illinois River was quite memorable to those who happened to be on the waterfront in early January 1943. In spite of an attempt to keep the move secret, on Saturday, Jan. 2, at 6:30 p.m., spectators crowded the banks along the river at Ottawa to watch the *Minnesota* slowly move a floating dry dock containing the *USS Peto* under the Hilliard Bridge. About an hour later, the 500-foot tow, entered the lock at Starved Rock. By 9 p.m., the tow passed under the Shippingsport Bridge with a Coast Guard cutter leading the way.

Twenty sailors, together with the entire Peru police force, were stationed along the banks to keep the curious spectators from getting too close. However, only a small crowd of about 100 people were down at the Peru waterfront to catch a glimpse of the first submarine to arrive at Peru. Rounding the bend east of the Peru bridge, the dry dock swung with the swift current. It took the tow boat *Minnesota* a half hour to get the dry dock moving into the north channel.

The tow was finally moored to take on supplies. Some spectators found that the 27-foot wings of the dry dock were so high that the submarine was difficult to see, but a flood light helped illuminate the conning tower and deck gun. By 10 p.m., the tow had cast off and was proceeding around the Peru swing bridge, which had been open since Oct. 1 while repairs were made.

The sailors faced rough water ahead as high winds and storms buffeted the tow on the trip down the Mississippi. The *USS Peto* arrived at a port facility near New Orleans on Jan. 7. This was just the first of 28 submarines, built at the Manitowoc Shipbuilding Co. that was floated down the Illinois River. *(Note - During WWII, the USS Peto was awarded 8 battlestars for action in the Pacific.)*

While the *USS Peto* was heading down to New Orleans, Cpl. Stanley Debosik, USMC, son of Mr. and Mrs. Peter Debosik, returned to his Oglesby home at 237 First St. with a different submarine story. He was involved with the sub-launched raid on

Makin Island in the Gilberts. During an interview with a reporter from the LaSalle *Post-Tribune*, published on Jan. 7, 1943, he described the Aug. 17, 1942 attack on the Japanese-occupied island. Cpl. Debosik, was one of 200 Marines who were taken to Makin Island on two submarines, the USS *Argonaut* and the USS *Nautilus*. Most of the men, Debosik included, were crammed into the *Argonaut*, which had all torpedoes removed except for the ones in the torpedo tubes to give the men more room. He said the heat was stifling, and many men were seasick.

The USS *Argonaut* (pictured) was accompanied by the USS *Nautilus* in the raid on Makin Island. US Navy photo.

Lt. Col. Evans Carlson was the commander of the raiders with Major James Roosevelt, son of President Franklin Roosevelt, as second in command of the raiders. On Aug. 17, rubber boats were launched from the subs. Debosik said, "The island was a seaplane base, and our attack came as a complete surprise. Landing on the beach, we immediately formed for the attack and in two hours time had everything in readiness. The entire group of 360 Japanese soldiers was killed during the 44 hours of fighting that followed with 23 of our marines being killed and 26 of us wounded, including myself."

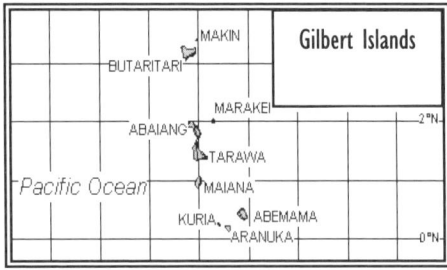

(Note - Carlson said that he counted the bodies of 83 Japanese and 14 Marines. Official casualty figures currently say that 18 Marines died; 12 were missing – 9 of whom were captured and later executed).

The raiders found that the Japanese had seized a couple of Chevy cars on the island and even smoked American cigarettes. According to Debosik, Japanese Zeros, bombers, and seaplanes attacked his unit seven times following the American assault. During the furious fighting, Debosik was wounded in the knee. The Marines withdrew after a day, rowing back to the submarines through heavy seas. The surprise attack was not meant to hold the island indefinitely but rather to destroy enemy supplies and gather intelligence. Stories like this inspired those on the home front.

Oglesby's Cpl. Stanley Debosik was among Carlson's Raiders when they returned from the raid on Makin Island. US Navy photo.

Delayed news of another battle in the Pacific distressed other families in the Illinois Valley. It wasn't until January 1943, that the navy released details of the fighting off the Santa Cruz Islands on Oct. 26. The aircraft carrier *USS Hornet* was badly damaged by bombs and torpedoes. It would be some time before Mr. and Mrs. Albert Flohr of Princeton could be sure that their son, Boatswain Mate Donald Flohr, was safe. Several months after the encounter, it was learned that Flohr, who manned a 20mm gun on the *USS Hornet*, was one of the survivors when the ship was sunk on Oct. 26, 1942.

The cruiser *USS Northampton* came to assist the stricken carrier during the Japanese aerial attack. Boatswain Mate Frank Rady, son of Mr. and Mrs. Joseph Rady of LaSalle, was a crewman on the *Northampton*. In a Feb. 2005 interview, Rady said many of the badly burned sailors from the *Hornet* were taken aboard the cruiser. Contrary to information given to the press, the *Northampton* was not sunk in the Santa Cruz battle. The LaSalle sailor said that his ship was not lost until the Battle of

Tassafaronga when the cruiser was part of the task force that attacked the Japanese forces near Guadalcanal on Nov. 30, 1942. In that engagement, the cruiser was hit by two torpedoes from the *Kwawkaze* and lost three of her four screws. The fires burning amidships made it impossible to save the ship so the captain ordered, "Abandon ship!"

USS Northampton at Brisbane, Australia Aug. 5, 1941. Note the camouflage wake line painted on the hull. US Navy photo.

A Japanese "Kate" (circled) flies over the *Hornet* after dropping a torpedo in the Battle of the Santa Cruz Islands on Oct. 26, 1942. Fragments of anti-aircraft shells splash in the water. US Navy photo.

The *USS Northampton* takes the *USS Hornet* in tow trying to save the carrier. According to Frank Rady, who was aboard the *Northampton*, the tow line to the badly damaged *Hornet* had to be cast off so that the cruiser could maneuver during a subsequent attack by the Japanese. The continued attacks on the *Hornet* resulted in the sinking of the carrier. US Navy photo.

Sometime after the loss of his ship, Seaman Rady was given a furlough and returned to see his parents. He recalled how he was first greeted by LaSalle store owner Louis Kosem who expressed his surprise saying, "Frankie Rady, you're not dead?" Confusing reports made it very difficult for families worried about their sons and daughters on distant battlefields.

A few days later, the LaSalle paper reported that Lt. C.R. Johnson of Princeton was safe. The ship to which he was assigned, the *USS Porter,* had been sunk by the Japanese submarine I-12 in the battle of the Santa Cruz Islands.

USS Porter. US Navy photo.

Much had changed since the bombing of Pearl Harbor. Many of the factory workers had been called by the Selective Service and were serving stateside at American camps, posts, and bases. Other servicemen and women were on the high seas and at the front lines throughout Europe, Africa, and Asia. On the home front, rationing, bond sales, and salvage drives became commonplace. War industries turned out the weapons and other necessities needed for the troops, and farmers were called upon to increase production.

In order to plan agricultural output, L.E. Leigh, chairman of the Marshall-Putnam Agricultural Adjustment Administration, designated Jan. 13 as "M" Day. The "M" stood for Mobilization. AAA committeemen were expected to meet in Henry to get their paperwork for area farmers to set their production goals. In order to receive government payments, farmers had to agree to meet 90 percent of the wheat production goals.

The Green River Ordnance Plant near Amboy continued to turn out munitions in ever-increasing numbers. The 155mm shells and 1600 pound bombs had been in production since mid-December 1942, and Line 7 was ready to open at the end of January for the production of rockets.

Green River workers stack the projectiles encased in protective tubes. Paulsen collection.

Nothing seemed to slow production at the Amboy plant until Jan. 19, 1943, when half of the workers never clocked in. A blizzard swept through northern Illinois as temperatures dropped to 10 degrees below zero. Drifting snow, caused by the high winds, closed many roads. A bus from the Oglesby Motor Transportation Co. left at midnight for Amboy and picked up 17 workers along the route from Oglesby to Spring Valley and Ladd. Bucking the high winds, the bus stalled in a drift north of Ladd at 2 a.m. Fortunately, the GROP workers were able to find shelter in a local farmhouse for the night. The next morning, a snowplow set out to open the road. It was followed by another bus to rescue the workers, but the bus did not reach the stranded workers until 2 p.m. A Central Trailways bus gave up trying to reach Amboy in the morning but was finally able to get through the snow drifts in the afternoon. Other buses heading east managed to get to the Elwood Ordnance Plant near Wilmington. Such weather-related problems were exceptional, and munitions production generally had few delays.

In spite of the sub-zero temperatures, about 300 farmers traveled to Ladd on Jan. 19 for a meeting sponsored by the Ladd businessmen regarding hemp production. One of the speakers, Father Joseph Brons from St. Benedict's Church, called upon the farmers to do their patriotic duty and establish "God's Acre." According to the *Post-Tribune* account, Father Joseph said that the product (hemp) would indirectly further God's plan to aid the country in its fight for decency and humanity. Another speaker from the University of Illinois said that the seed being made available for the 1943 season was produced in Kentucky since foreign seed produced poor crops. It was hoped that many of the farmers would sign hemp contracts with the government.

While adults were busy with their jobs, school children were challenged with a new project to support the military. Margaret O'Brien was in charge of the collection of silk and nylon stockings for gunpowder bags. By Jan. 21, St. Hyacinth's school led all of the elementary schools by collecting 3,470 stockings. St. Patrick's followed with 1,326. That total, combined with the stockings collected at St. Joseph's, St. Roch's, Jefferson, Washington, Matthiessen, Campbell, Lincoln, and Jackson elementary schools and the L-P High School total of 3,814 stockings, brought the grand total to over 11,000 stockings. Miss O'Brien was gratified by the outstanding work of the students noting that it required 30 stockings to make one bag of high explosives. By the end of the month, St. Hyacinth's added another 1,300 bringing the total for the month to almost 16,000 stockings. Three stores in LaSalle, Reardon's, Blakely's, and Penny's, also had collection boxes, but it was the children that turned in the highest numbers.

Streator was noted for several major contributions to the war effort. One factory, the Anthony Hydraulic Co., received contracts for the manufacture of bomb carriers and trailers. The carriers made the job of moving and loading the heaviest bombs to the bomb bays of a variety of aircraft much easier. The outstanding production at the Streator plant was recognized on Jan. 22, 1943. Capt. Robert Henderson, representing the chief of naval operations, presented Mr. L.E. Walker with the coveted Army-Navy "E" pennant. Employees were given commemorative, blue and white caps to wear for the presentation. Streatorland Historical Society.

Almost 2,000 Anthony Co. workers gathered for the presentation of the "E" pennant. Mrs. Etta Bellis of the special body department and George Pouk of the welding shop were selected as employees' representatives to receive "E" pins. *Shop Talk.*

Raising the "E" flag at the Anthony plant. *Shop Talk.*

As the ceremony concluded, Anthony's woodshop foreman, William C. Schroeder, presented a Navy representative with a Mark II trailer as a donation from the workers.

Navy Lt. R.T. Tiebout accepted the trailer saying, "It will serve to good advantage in the Pacific War Zone, and you have the thanks of the men who use it." The Anthony Co. was the first factory in LaSalle County to receive the Army-Navy "E" Award.

Meanwhile, the Peru city council was anxiously awaiting the completion of the Honor Roll sign recognizing its men in the military. On Jan. 29, the 36-foot long sign was finally completed by Otto Karlosky and installed on the Welland Building. There were over 600 names arranged alphabetically with the inscription, "United We Stand," in the center of the 8-foot high sign. A painting of a soldier and a sailor flanked the 12 panels of names. Anxious to illustrate Peru's support for its servicemen, the city council voted in February to have a postcard reproduction of the sign created so that residents could send a picture of the honor roll to military personnel.

In early February, Illinois Valley residents began to be affected by OPA's new gas rationing rules. One change, effective Feb 1, eliminated all charge purchases. Now, only cash payments were acceptable. The new OPA regulation was designed to help service station owners eliminate some of the required paperwork.

The operators themselves had to contend with another regulation that restricted them to a 72-hour week. Every station in LaSalle, Peru, Oglesby, and Utica was closed on Sundays, so they could be open 12 hours the other days of the week. Owners could determine their individual operating hours so long as they did not sell gas to "A," "B," or "C" purchasers more than 12 hours in a 24-hour period. Truckers and taxis with their "T" books could get gas beyond those time constraints.

It was not until February that the WPB authorized clock production at Westclox. Typical runs required 300 pounds of brass for every 1000 clocks. However, because of shortages, new clock designs would have to be drastically altered to cut brass usage to 10 pounds per 1000 clocks, according to information released in the company's *Tick Talk* magazine. Westclox management even considered constructing the cases out of molded paper. In any event, a new design was in the planning stages, and clock production could resume.

Bond sales, especially through the payroll deduction system, were gaining in popularity in the Tri-Cities. Gus Charles, chairman of the local United Mine Workers war bond committee, announced on Feb. 6 that the coal miners at the Union Coal Co. had agreed "100 percent 10 percent." At a minimum, each worker had 10¢ of every dollar of his paycheck deducted to buy defense bonds. As a result, a blue and white "Minute Man" was now flying directly beneath the Stars and Stripes on the company flagpole.

Rationing affected more people every day. Tuesday, Feb. 9, marked the beginning of nationwide shoe rationing. The shortage of leather, mainly due to the consumption of 1/3 of the available supply by the military, prompted the unexpected announcement from Washington.

The rules were spelled out by the OPA. There were no limits set for house slippers, infants' soft-soled shoes, and rubber boots, nor was any restriction placed on having old shoes repaired. But evening slippers, spiked shoes, and patent leather shoes were now banned from future production. Coupon No. 17 in the old sugar ration book was going to be used to allow three pairs of shoes a year. The effect of the announcement was mainly noted in larger cities where shoe stores were mobbed with shoppers trying to buy extra shoes before the regulation went into effect.

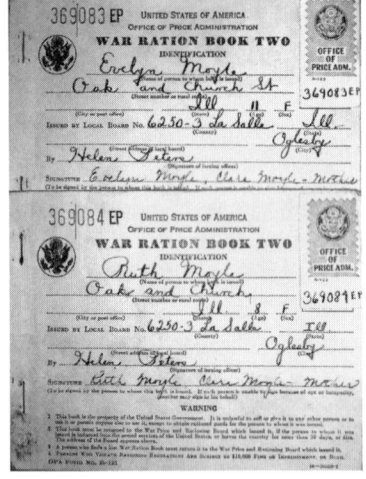

Every member of the family was entitled to a War Ration Book. Pictured are the books issued to Evelyn Moyle (11) and Ruth Moyle (8). Oglesby Library.

There was no shortage of jobs in the Illinois Valley during the war. Margarette Faletti of Granville was typical of many female workers at Westclox. She worked on artillery shell fuses for a time, but she lost her job when she married a returning serviceman. Westclox had a policy of neither hiring nor keeping married women on the job because of increased insurance cost.

With the high demand for labor, Mrs. Faletti had no trouble finding another position. She was hired immediately by the Sampsel Time Control Co. in Spring Valley as a lathe operator. With her experience at Westclox, she was quickly turning out fuse caps for navy torpedoes. Husbands and wives quickly found work at Sampsel's. Gladys Holman of Cedar Point assembled armatures and later became an inspector of coil windings. Her husband, Orpha, was an inspector and in charge of the tool crib.

(Note-The Holman children joined their parents at the plant during the Korean War. While still enrolled at L-P High School, Martha (Holman) Yauch, earned as much as 75 cents an hour at Sampsel's soldering electrical harnesses needed by the air corps. Her brother, Gene, worked in the accounting department.)

Company President Arthur V. Sampsel was eager to promote the military by hosting an exhibit of a navy 20mm anti-aircraft gun on Feb. 17. He said, "The stop by the navy crew is one of 125 being made at industrial plants which manufacture parts of the weapon or ammunition fired by it." Sampsel's 300 employees, together with several hundred other adults and students from Oglesby, LaSalle, Peru, DePue, and Spring Valley schools, had an opportunity to listen to an explanation of the gun's operation. During the program, the Sampsel Hep-Cat Band played an appropriate tune, "Praise the Lord and Pass the Ammunition."

The Depression years had fostered the development of many innovative programs to train young people for practical jobs. The National Youth Administration (NYA) was still offering courses in Peru for local applicants, ages 16-24. Free training plus pay resulted in many jobs during the war. For example, Mary Grosjean and Jean Zant of Peru and Florence Entwistle from LaSalle completed the 160 hours of training and became lathe operators at the Sampsel Co. Another graduate of the NYA program was Francis Affelt of Peru, who was hired as a machine operator at the Seneca shipyard.

With a constant demand for metal, the government called on everyone to search for more scrap. Tony Potocnik, manager of the Aida Theater in Oglesby, received the support of School Supt. J. Richard Evans, in a cooperative effort in which the children could bring copper, bronze, or brass to school in exchange for a free matinee ticket on Monday, Feb. 22.

Like LaSalle County, many towns in Bureau County had sponsored metal drives before. Princeton decided to join in the campaign by sponsoring an effort to pick up tin cans throughout the city on Feb. 26-27.

One would think the American armed forces had all the guns they needed, but that was apparently not the case. The Peru American Legion learned that extra weapons would be useful in navy training program at Great Lakes. The post organized a firearms collection campaign, which paid off with the donation of various small arms and rifles. The Polish Falcons Lodge of St. Valentine's Church, represented by Vincent Ratkiewicz, John Jakubek and Martin Dekowsky, donated a collection of 34 Springfield rifles and bayonets that their drill team had used. Father Simon Bernardi of Holy Rosary Church even donated his German Mauser pistol. Several .32 caliber revolvers and ammunition came from other donors. By the middle of March, the weapons collected in the "Guns for Navy" program totaled 38 rifles and 11 revolvers. Lt. Maley from the Great Lakes Training Center came to Peru on Mar. 16 to formally accept the arms.

While well-intentioned, some of the regulations coming from Washington turned out to be short-sighted. One example of bureaucratic nonsense was the decision to ban sliced bread. Bakeries in the Illinois Valley and throughout the rest of the country were told to stop slicing bread for customers so there would be less demand for new bread-slicing machines. The other reason for the ban was that someone in the WPB bureaucracy figured out that there would be less wax-paper needed to wrap unsliced bakery bread than sliced bread. It took two months of debate and haggling in Washington before Food Administrator Claude Wickard relented and rescinded the ludicrous regulation.

First it was tires and sugar; then gas and shoes. What would the government need to ration next? The word soon came that on Feb. 20, the sale of canned fruits and vegetables would stop, at least temporarily, so grocers could take inventories of their supplies before rationing began. Registration for new ration books was about to begin. Homemakers were told to take an inventory of all their canned goods since they would have to file a declaration of all their canned vegetables and fruits in excess of five cans per person. The good news was that the supply of coffee had increased in February, exceeding estimates by 20 percent. OPA decided to allow Ration Stamp No. 26, used for coffee purchases, to be valid until April 25 – several weeks longer than the previously announced expiration date. About the only items not rationed were milk, cereals, fresh fruit and vegetables, bakery goods, and relishes. The complete list of unrestricted foods would not be known until the end of March. In the meantime, there was a rush to the local schools to register for Ration Book Two.

With the prospect of more food rationing, Dave Malone, chairman of the Oglesby Victory Garden program, encouraged every family to plant a garden to raise vegetables for family use. In 1942, Oglesby had 545 victory gardens. Malone hoped that the number would climb to at least 600 for the coming spring and said he was willing to donate packages of pepper seeds from his prize-winning garden. Mayor Moyle pointed out that there would be no garden space available on city property but suggested that those who wanted to start a garden should try to use the numerous vacant lots in Oglesby.

Oglesby wasn't alone in the effort to get people involved in planting a vegetable garden. The LaSalle PTA met on Mar. 9 to review a suggestion proposed by School Supt. E.J. Miller. There was a 10-acre plot of land north of the Matthiessen School that the school board offered to the public for this purpose. Edward Kasprowicz, chairman of victory gardens for the LaSalle defense council, made it known that there was space for 90 gardens on the Matthiessen school grounds alone.

As the spring planting season approached, additional areas were identified by the City of LaSalle for those who wanted to raise vegetables. One six-acre plot was located near St. Mary's Hospital, and another location was west of the new Electrical Utilities factory. The city was even willing to plow the land at its own expense to make the planting a little easier. Over 75 applications had been made to use the free land. Approximately ten additional acres were made available west of the Peru city limits. Carl Struever, general manager of American Nickeloid, announced that the employees would be encouraged to raise vegetables on company-owned land. According to the company magazine, the *Nickelodian*, "It's not only fun but profitable too."

Area libraries continued to collect books for servicemen. Mrs. Walter May of the Matson Public Library in Princeton reported that the collection effort in their Victory Book Drive had been a success; 600 books had been donated including 241 from Buda and another 205 from Princeton.

The home front was constantly receiving information about the war from servicemen returning home. MM1c Earl Willmeroth was on the *USS Vestal,* when the Japanese attacked on Dec. 7th. He shared his experiences with his parents, Mr. and Mrs. Herman Willmeroth of Peru. He said that he had some minor burns when he was thrown into water covered with burning oil after a bomb exploded nearby in the first attack. During the second attack, he took refuge under a nearby box car. Only later did he learn that the car was loaded with ammunition.

USS Vestal, a repair ship, was beached after the Dec. 7 attack.
US Navy photo.

The local American Legion and VFW posts didn't want to forget men like Willmeroth so they did what they could to record their sacrifices and make homecomings as pleasant as possible. In Spring Valley, veterans purchased the Doyle barber shop and turned it into their first permanent American Legion home. It was to be a place where veterans of all conflicts could readjust themselves. Spring Valley VFW Post No. 3666 decided to erect an

honor roll board (at left) in the Spring Valley city park to list all of city's WWII veterans, which by March 1943 numbered close to 500.

LaSalle *Daily Post-Tribune*, Mar. 20, 1943.

On Mar. 20, 1943, the LaSalle *Post-Tribune* published its second special wartime edition describing the events of the previous year. Hundreds of photos and stories of the men and women who were stationed around the world and at camps in the United States were included. The efforts of home front industries, churches, civic groups, and social organizations were not overlooked. Every town from Marseilles to Mendota; LaSalle to Ladd; Dalzell to DePue; and everywhere in between had sections of the paper devoted to the salvage drives, Red Cross programs, American Legion and VFW functions, and factory bond sales. Secrecy prevented publication of the amount and description of war production, but companies, large and small, proudly featured their service banners with ads illustrating their continuing efforts to help win the war, both on the production lines and by bond purchases. Ads from LaSalle *Post-Tribune*, Mar. 20, 1943.

The return of a serviceman was typically a joyous occasion for family and friends. On May 7, Capt. Maurice Bishop of the Army Air Corps was flying cross country from Cleveland, OH in an army trainer. Bishop, a graduate of Princeton H.S. and West Point, decided to make a stop to visit his parents, Mr. and Mrs. A. Ray Parker in Princeton on the way. Before making a landing at Dixon, he decided to give Princeton residents a thrill by circling the city several times.

Photo-Capt. Bishop, *Bureau County Republican,* May 11, 1943.

It was his first visit home in two years. He had been serving as commandant of cadets at Roswell, NM. After his brief stay, he climbed into the cockpit and flew off to an undisclosed location.

The *Bureau County Republican* often used letters and personal interviews from returning servicemen to convey dramatic episodes in the war to its readers. One such story described a thrilling encounter when an American plane spotted a Nazi sub in the South Atlantic. Russell Gernhofer, son of Florence Gernhofer of Princeton, related his experience as a gunner on a PBY, flying anti-submarine missions in the South Atlantic. He said, they spotted a U-boat running on the surface and dove on the boat.

(Photo- US Navy PBY)

They came so close to the sub that they could see the expressions on the faces of the German sailors as the American crew opened fire. Although the boat crash dived, it was too late. The PBY dropped its bombs, straddling the sub; the explosions apparently ruptured the hull. The sub was last seen sinking stern first as the PBY flew overhead.

The folks in Malden were eager to read the story of one of their home town heroes, Everett Gustafson. He was a tail gunner on a B-17 Flying Fortress with the 26th Heavy Bomber Squadron. In one aerial encounter, a Japanese plane was firing at his plane with 7.7 mm rounds when one hit just behind his seat. He brought the exploded shell home as evidence of his story. Gustafson was awarded a Purple Heart and three Air Service Medals.

Another local veteran returning in the spring of '43 with a harrowing story was GM3c Franklin Pierce of Bureau. He was a gunner aboard a merchant ship when it was torpedoed in the Atlantic in October 1942. He was one of the few survivors.

While there were numerous stories of dangerous and daring military encounters, not everyone was fortunate enough to return home to tell their stories shortly after the events took place. For example, Lt. Donald "Gene" Whipple, son of Mr. and Mrs. J.J. Whipple of Princeton, a graduate of Princeton H.S. Class of '37, was one of the pilots flying a bombing mission over Bremen, Germany in the spring of 1943. The Americans came under heavy attack, and 20 of the bombers, including Lt. Whipple's plane, were shot down. Initially, he was reported missing, but later on June 17, news was received in Princeton that he was a German POW.

While these stories brought the war closer to home for hundreds of Illinois Valley families, it was the little sacrifices that touched the lives of everyone. On Mar. 29, 1943, rationing was expanded to include all meats, cheeses, shortenings, salad oils, butter, margarine, and canned fish. According to the guidelines announced by the Putnam County War Price and Ration Board, the amounts allowed would correspond with Ration Book Two. An elaborate point system was devised to ensure an equitable distribution of limited foods. A total of 81 points in red stamps were allotted for each person in April. Farm families, who raised much of their own food, were encouraged not to use any of the red ration stamps. Farmers were also responsible for collecting ration stamps if they sold any of their farm-raised products.

OFFICIAL TABLE OF CONSUMER POINT VALUES FOR MEAT, FATS, FISH, AND CHEESE
No. 1—Effective March 29, 1943

COMMODITY	Points per lb.	COMMODITY	Points per lb.	COMMODITY	Points per lb.	COMMODITY	Points per lb.	COMMODITY	Points per lb.
BEEF		**BEEF**		**LAMB—MUTTON**		**PORK**		**READY-TO-EAT MEATS**	
STEAKS		VARIETY MEATS		STEAKS AND CHOPS		STEAKS AND CHOPS		COOKED, BOILED, BAKED, AND BARBECUED	
Porterhouse	8	Brains	3	Loin Chops	8	Center Chops	8	Dried Beef	12
T-Bone	8	Hearts	4	Rib Chops	7	End Chops	7	Ham—bone in, whole or half	9
Club	8	Kidneys	3	Leg Chops	6	Loin—boneless, fresh or cured only	10	Ham—bone in, slices	11
Rib—10-inch cut	7	Livers	6	Shoulder Chops—blade or arm chops	4	Tenderloin	10	Ham—butt or shank end	9
Rib—7-inch cut	8	Sweetbreads	4			Ham, slices	8	Ham—boneless, whole or half	
Sirloin	8	Tails (or joints)	3	ROASTS		Shoulder Chops and Steaks	7	Ham—boneless, slices	10
Sirloin—boneless	9	Tongues	6	Leg—whole or part	6	Bellies, fresh and cured only	6	Picnic or Shoulder—bone in	11
Round	8	Tripe	3	Sirloin Roast—bone in	6			Picnic or Shoulder—boneless	6
Bottom Round	8			Yoke, Rattle, or Triangle—bone in	5	ROASTS		Bouillon Cubes, Beef Extract, and all other meat extracts and concentrates	10
Round Tip	8	**VEAL**		Yoke, Rattle, or Triangle—boneless	6	Loin—whole, half, or end cuts	7	Tongues	7
Chuck or Shoulder	7			Chuck or Shoulder, square cut—bone in	4	Loin—center cuts	8	Spareribs	6
Flank	8	STEAKS AND CHOPS		Chuck or Shoulder, square cut—boneless	6	Ham—whole or half	7	Pigs Feet—bone in	2
		Loin Chops	8	Chuck or Shoulder, cross cut—bone in	3	Ham—butt or shank end	7	The point value of any other ready-to-eat meat item shall be determined by adding 2 points per pound to the point value per pound of the uncooked item from which it is prepared if it is sold whole, or 3 points per pound shall be added if it is cooked and sliced.	
ROASTS		Rib Chops	7			Ham—shank half (picnic) bone in	6		
Rib—standing (chine bone on) (10" cut)	7	Shoulder Chops	6	STEWS AND OTHER CUTS		Shoulder—shank half (picnic) boneless	8		
Rib—standing (chine bone on) (10" cut)		Round Steak (cutlets)	8	Breast and Flank	3	Shoulder—butt half (Boston butt)—bone in	7		
Blade Rib—standing (chine bone on) (7" cut)	6	Sirloin Steak or Chops	7	Neck—bone in	4	Shoulder—butt half (Boston butt)—boneless	8		
Blade Rib—standing (chine bone on) (7" cut)	8	ROASTS		Neck—boneless	6			**SAUSAGE**	
Round Tip		Rump and Sirloin—bone in	6	Shank—bone in	4	OTHER PORK CUTS			
Rump—bone in	7	Rump and Sirloin—boneless	8	Lamb Patties—lamb ground from necks, flanks, shanks, breasts and miscellaneous lamb trimmings	5	Spareribs	4	Dry Sausage—Hard: Typical items are hard Salami, hard Cervelat, and Pepperoni	9
Rump—boneless	8	Shoulder—bone in	7			Neck and Backbones	2		
Chuck or Shoulder—bone in	6	Shoulder—boneless	8			Plates, regular	5		
Chuck or Shoulder—boneless	7			VARIETY MEATS		Feet—bone in	1	Semi-dry Sausage: Typical items are soft Salami, Thuringer, and Mortadella	8
		STEWS AND OTHER CUTS		Brains	3	Fat Backs and Clear Plates	4		
STEWS AND OTHER CUTS		Breast—bone in	4	Hearts	3	Hocks and Knuckles	3		
Short Ribs	4	Flank Meat	5	Kidneys	2	Jowls	5	Fresh, Smoked and Cooked Sausage:	
Plate—bone in	4	Neck—bone in	4	Sweetbreads	4	Leaf Fat	4	Group A: Typical items are Pork Sausage, Wieners, Bologna, Baked Loaves, and Liver Sausage	7
Plate—boneless	5	Neck—boneless	6	Tongues	4				
Brisket—bone in	4	Shank—bone in	4			VARIETY MEATS			
Brisket—boneless	6	Shank and Heel Meat—boneless	6	**BACON**		Brains	3		
Flank Meat	5	Ground Veal and Patties—veal ground from necks, flanks, shanks, breasts and miscellaneous veal trimmings	5	Bacon—slab or piece, rind on	5	Chitterlings	4	Group B: Typical items are Scrapple and Tamales, Souse and Head Cheese also included	4
Neck—bone in	5			Bacon—slab or piece, rind off	6	Hearts	3		
Neck—boneless	6			Bacon—sliced, rind off	8	Kidneys	2		
Heel of Round—boneless	6			Bacon—Canadian style, piece or sliced	11	Livers	5		
Shank—bone in	4	VARIETY MEATS		Bacon—rinds	1	Tongues	6		
Shank—boneless	6	Brains	4	Bacon—plate and jowl squares	6	Ears	1		
HAMBURGER		Hearts	5			Tails	3		
Beef ground from necks, flanks, shanks, briskets, plates, and miscellaneous beef trimmings and beef fat	5	Kidneys	3			Snouts	2		
		Livers	6						
		Sweetbreads	4						
		Tongues	6						

Tables were published so that consumers knew exactly how many points were required for food purchases beginning on Mar. 29, 1943. *PC Record.*

In anticipation of the meat rationing, shoppers in some local groceries bought everything in the coolers the day before rationing began. Markets were "sold out to the walls." In spite of the heavy buying earlier, once official rationing began on Mar. 29, stores were more crowded than usual for a Monday. Shoppers carefully added up the required points and stamps. For every pound of meat, cheese, and lard, two red stamps had to be removed from Ration Book Two and turned over to the grocer.

Washington bureaucrats tried to explain the reasons for nationwide meat rationing. Many people, who had been unemployed during the Depression, now had jobs and were spending the extra money on steaks, chops, and roasts. Women had entered the workforce, and the hard manual labor created appetites not easily satisfied with low calorie meals. Then too, there was the obvious demand by the government, which not only had to build up reserves to feed the thousands of armed forces personnel, but also meet the demands created by the Lend-Lease program supplying the Allies. Another major factor was that the supply of meat was being siphoned off by black market sales, which some reports said was as bad as bootlegged alcohol. "Meatlegging" was the term used by some reporters.

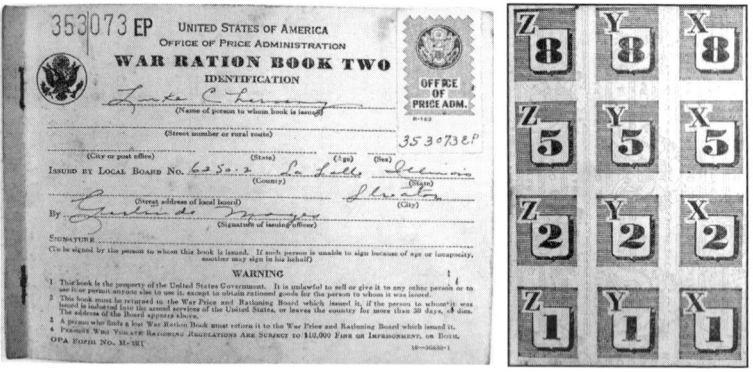

War Ration Book Two contained coupons numbered 1-2-5-8, a mathematical combination suitable for a variety of purchasing transactions. Deadlines for the use of the coupons were printed in the local papers, but sometimes not every coupon was redeemed. Streator Historical Society.

While housewives were counting points and totaling ration stamps, the school children in LaSalle were busy buying war savings stamps for the "Buy a Jeep" campaign. The US Treasury promised a citation for every school that purchased $900 worth of stamps by April 19. That amount represented the cost of one army jeep. Typically, every Tuesday was the day to buy stamps at school. To stimulate sales, there was a special "April Fool" sale, advertised with caricatures of Hitler, Mussolini, and Hirohito printed on handbills. The last day of the campaign, April 19, was designated as "Minute Man Day." Any school that had a 90-percent student participation rate for stamps sales during April would be allowed to fly the Minute Man flag in front of their school. This was considered a great honor.

The students at L-P-O Junior College showed their support of former students, who had been called to duty in the armed forces, by erecting a plaque near the main office of the college. A brief ceremony was held on April 7. The names of 129 former L-P-O students were engraved on metal plates attached to the leather-covered plaque. Mary Bassett of Oglesby explained the purpose of the plaque. The ceremony continued with Miss Marion Smith of Spring Valley leading the student body in the recitation of the Pledge of Allegiance, which was followed by the singing of the "Star Spangled Banner."

Patriotic ceremonies filled the hearts of parents and spouses of those in the armed forces with pride, but at the same time, families lived in apprehension of the sight of Western Union messengers coming to the door. The sad news came on Sunday, May 2, to Matt Skutt, a farmer in Hennepin Township. His 22-year old son, Edward, had been killed in North Africa on April 8, 1943. He was the first wartime casualty in Putnam County.

After many long months of negotiating with area farmers, the federal government announced in early April that a deal had been finalized to secure the commitments needed to cultivate and process hemp in the area. John Bartoli from Cherry had agreed to sell the government 80 acres of his land in Ladd. During the summer of 1943, Bartoli would be allowed to plant a small grain crop on 74 acres with the understanding that the fields would be vacated by Sept. 1. Only six acres of the farmland would be needed initially to build the hemp processing facility. The rest of the acreage would be used for stacking hemp straw in the fall. Other hemp processing plants would be built at Earlville, Wyoming, and Minonk

With shortages of sugar facing housewives, who normally canned fruit, plans had to be made to secure canning sugar applications in mid-May. Rationing boards needed the information to determine how much sugar could be allocated when they distributed ration books on August 15. The plan would be very much like the previous year except that there would be a more generous allotment available with a top limit of 25 pounds of sugar per person. In order to pick up a new ration book, Book One had to be presented, and the total number of quarts or pounds of finished fruits to be processed had to be specified.

During the spring of 1943, the government was already preparing for the summertime distribution of Ration Book Three. The four inside pages of the eight-page booklet had 48 unit stamps for the purchase of items like sugar and coffee. The other four pages were printed with point stamps similar to those used in Ration Book Two. Applications for Book Three were sent through the mail beginning May 20. The plan was to use the new book to replace Books One and Two, but not to add new items to the rationed list. When War Ration Book Three was issued, the government changed the design of the stamps. Now pictured were the weapons of war, tanks, cannons, aircraft carriers, and planes. The different numbers on the 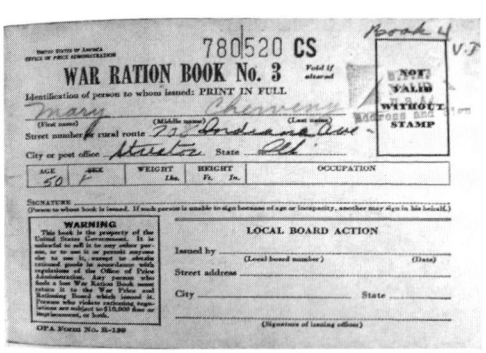 stamps corresponded to different items on the ration list. For example, in Ration Book One, coupon No. 12 was needed to buy 5 lbs. of sugar. Coupon No. 17 was the shoe coupon, and coupon No. 23 had to be turned in to buy a pound of coffee.

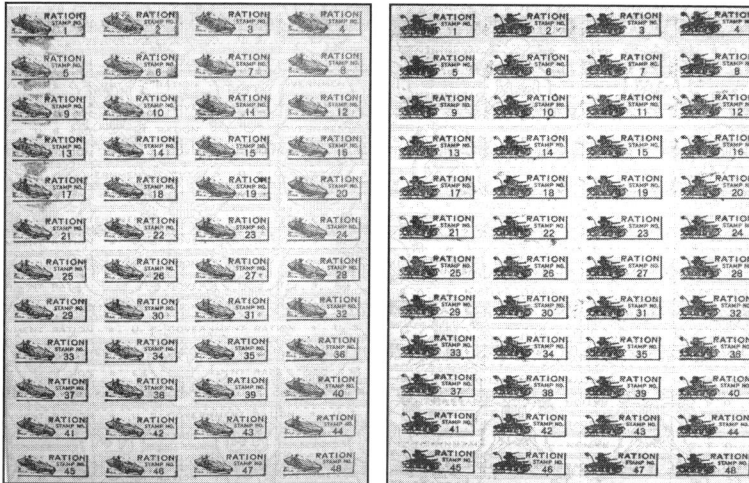

War Ration Book Number Three stamp pages. Streatorland Historical Society.

Rationing may have been a bureaucratic challenge at the national and local levels, but it also allowed for a fair distribution of the available supplies and controlled prices. Once rationing was in effect, prices on meat rose only slightly. According to the Department of Labor Statistics, round steak and chuck roast went from 44.2¢/lb. in May 1942 to 45.3¢/lb. in Feb. 1943. Potatoes, which jumped from 23¢ for ten pounds in August 1939 to 35¢ in May 1942, had dropped to only 19¢ in Feb. 1943.

Victory Gardeners in the Tri-Cities were encouraged in their work when the local ration board determined that such individuals could use a little extra gas to tend their plots. It was decided that individuals who had gardens of at least 1,500 sq. ft. would be issued a "B" sticker allowing enough fuel for an extra 300 miles of travel each month.

The system of gas rationing and tire recycling had developed some problems. Service stations were accepting "loose" ration coupons instead of meeting the requirement that coupons could only be removed only by the filling station attendant. A meeting with C.H. Padgett, OPA regulator from Peoria, and 75 local gas station owners and tire inspectors at the Hotel Kaskaskia in the summer of '43 was meant to serve as a warning not to relax the rules. Because of a growing black market trade in gas stamps, managers were cautioned to make sure that the name and automobile registration on the coupon book corresponded with the license number of the car driven to the station.

Padgett also warned that enforcement inspectors would make frequent inspections, and owners in violation of the rules would be penalized. He said that 95 percent of the station operators wanted the regulations enforced. When station owners accepted the loose coupons, Padgett said, they were encouraging people to "give away or sell coupons they do not use, or obtain gasoline with coupons that have been stolen." Another OPA representative at the meeting, B.L. Eastburn, reminded tire inspectors to keep detailed records of trade-ins for new tires, making sure that certificates were not issued if a worn tire could be recapped.

The whole rationing system was in jeopardy by the summer of '43 because of the increasing work load on local OPA boards. What had started as a job that only took a few hours each week had turned into a bookkeeping nightmare. Volunteers for the rationing boards found that the responsibilities had created a full time job. Rationing board chairman Charles Miller said, "The work has fallen upon the shoulders of five or six members, some of them devoting six to eight hours a day of their time and effort. At times they have worked day and night, and now have reached a stage where it is physically impossible for these few members to carry on. Persons must be found in the Tri-Cities who are willing to serve the war effort. There must be no delay, and unless cooperation is received there is grave danger of a breakdown which would be a serious blow to this community and cause inconvenience and hardship to approximately 40,000 persons within the board's jurisdiction."

The rationing of metals had completely shut down the Big Ben clock production at Westclox, but the government soon realized that alarm clocks were still needed. So, the Westclox designers figured out a way to manufacture clocks with less metal. In May, Westclox announced that production would begin on a new model. The $1.65 clock, produced with only a small number of brass parts, would be available in small quantities. The clocks did not bear the Westclox name but were simply labeled "Waralarm" on the face. The black case was made from pressed wood fibers and was coated with black lacquer. The first models had a bell alarm, but later that was changed to a buzzer. The company asked that employees refrain from purchasing the model because of wartime shortages and WPB quotas.

Waralarm clock photo - *Tick Talk* magazine, May 1943.

While alarm clocks didn't seem to have a direct bearing on success at the front, other products made by Westclox did make a definite contribution. All sorts of fuses were needed to detonate various flares and shells. The M-26 parachute flare was one type of fuse manufactured at the Peru plant. Other fuses turned out for the armed forces were the 40mm anti-aircraft fuse, the M-48, M-52, MT T56 nose bomb fuse (pictured at right), the M-72, and the M-111 A2 flare fuses. Westclox workers also assembled parts for the navy's Mark XX primer, terminals for distributors on army aircraft, and parts for bomb sights.

Flares, equipped with Westclox fuses, were used extensively in the invasion of Sicily in July 1943. According to the company magazine, "The time fuse permits its use for high altitude bombardment. It may be made to function at 3,000 feet when released from aircraft at any altitude between 5,500 and 25,000 feet."

US Army photo of M-26 flares equipped with Westclox fuses published in the August 1943 edition of *Tick Talk* magazine.

Westclox products could turn up in the most unlikely places. Albert P. March of Peru, a graduate of LaSalle-Peru H.S. and former Westclox shipping clerk, joined the Army and was assigned to the 132nd infantry, 2nd Battalion. After seeing action in a number of the South Pacific islands, his unit was sent into the thick of fighting in Guadalcanal. He wrote home in May describing how he had occasion to see two other former Westclox employees, Louis Ryba and Frank Holsinger, members of the 1st Battalion. Even more interesting and ironic was a picture he found when rifling though the pockets of one of the dead Japanese soldiers. He wrote, "I was quite surprised and thrilled to find on his person a picture of himself seated behind a desk and a Big Ben staring right at me in the face. It sure made me think of the old factory and the good ole U.S.A."

Other young men were looking forward to joining the army. As the school year came to an end, the Officer Cadet Corps at Ottawa H.S. held its annual military drill demonstration at King Field. Army officers inspected the cadet corps, and the band played martial music.

Officers from Camp Ellis inspected the cadets in their execution of the manual of arms and in drill.

Officers from the regular US Army were impressed with the precision executed by the cadet corps at Ottawa H.S.

Photos from Ottawa H.S. 1944 Yearbook.

Few schools had a cadet corps like Ottawa H.S., but most schools were involved in a variety of programs to show their patriotism and understanding of the war. The Illinois State

Superintendent of Schools recommended that all schools observe "a day of mourning" on May 10, 1943. This was not to recognize the casualties of the war but rather an observance to mark the 10th anniversary of the day in 1933 when the Nazis publicly burned school textbooks and focused all teaching on a military-oriented curriculum. The LaSalle school superintendent agreed with the recommendation and directed that all school flags be flown at half mast to remind students of what the Nazis thought of traditional academics.

When participation in defense stamp sales at the Jefferson and Campbell schools reached 90 percent, the schools were rewarded with "Minute Man" flags. They had set a goal of $900, the price of an army jeep, and had exceeded that goal.

A formal flag dedication ceremony was held on Monday, May 17 at the Jefferson School. With the sounding of reveille at 9 a.m., the students assembled outside. Herbert Klein, Ron Confrey, Don Tidabeck, and Conrad Festa served as color guards. Part of the program involved Daniel Parsons presenting a "Jeep" citation. After a choral reading by the eighth graders, the program closed with the entire student body singing "God Bless America." The students were proud of their new banner bearing a dark blue "Minute Man" on a white field.

High school graduations took on a special significance that spring. The LaSalle-Peru H.S. Class of '43 had several special seniors present during its graduation ceremonies. On June 3, three of the 261 graduates were dressed in military uniforms instead of traditional caps and gowns. Ludwig Hrovat, and Lawrence Moellering had on their army uniforms while Ryan Cawley wore his navy uniform. The young men had enlisted before graduation but were able to be present to receive their diplomas. According to the *Post-Tribune*, other members of the class were also in the armed forces but couldn't be present. Charles Ambrose, Francis Jaruseski, Theodore Maciejewski, Tom Rosolia, and Albert Wieczorek were in the Navy. William Lister and Vincent Orlandini had enlisted in the Army Air Corps. Russell Meyer and John Kelly were in the Army. Walter Joop and Wayne Toellen were Marines. Frank Polcyn had joined the Coast Guard.

Reports on servicemen and women continued to fill every edition of the LaSalle *Post-Tribune*. One brief item described another first for women in the Tri-Cities. Florence Szydlowski from LaSalle passed all her exams and was waiting to be called for officer candidate school for the Marine Reserves.

Soldiers were able to get a furlough, especially when wounded or sick. When Sgt. Tom Eden of Bureau County returned, he brought with him a number of Japanese military artifacts collected after the Battle of Guadalcanal. During May 1943, they were put on display at the Putnam County State Bank in Hennepin. Some of the war souvenirs included a gas mask, a bayonet, a .25 caliber rifle, machine gun bullets, a trench mortar and even part of a Jap Zero.

It was recommended for young men not yet drafted and not employed in war production to seek jobs in war plants. The Seneca shipyard was the one place where many jobs were available. LST's 198 and 199 were completed in January and February 1943 and, after being fitted for sea duty, were turned over to the British navy. In March, three more LST's were commissioned. The pace continued as four more ships slid down the ways in April.

Mrs. Bernice Renkosik Neurohr, a worker in the timekeeping department at the yards, was suitably chosen for the christening honors on May 11 for LST 208. Her husband, Pfc John Neurohr of Ottawa, was stationed in England, and her father, Frank Renkosik Sr., and two brothers, Robert and Frank Jr. from LaSalle, worked on the ships at Seneca. Two other brothers, Benny and Edward Renkosik, were stationed overseas. The fast-paced work schedule did not allow for a grand ceremony, but those men and women who could not leave their jobs could hear the brief ceremony over the public address system. Frank Bazzoni, the shipyard photographer, recorded in his journal, "12th ship launched at 10 a.m. The weather–RAIN. Shipyard employees did not witness this launching – the first one without an audience."

Other ships followed quickly. At the end of May, LST 209 was launched. It was followed by LST 210 on June 1 and LST 211 on June 5.

Saturday, June 12, 1943, was a very special day for the shipyard. Approximately 10,000 guests and visitors gathered at the Seneca shipyard to view the presentation of the coveted Army-Navy "E" flag. Top executives of Chicago Bridge and Iron, the Navy Pier band, and officers for the US Navy had traveled to Seneca for the momentous occasion.

Capt. Wallace R. Dowd, USN, Supervisor of Shipbuilding, presented the Army-Navy "E" Award to George T. Horton, President of the Chicago Bridge and Iron Co. CBI, *Our Prairie Shipyard.*

Commenting on the importance of the LST production at Seneca, Admiral C.L. Brand said, "Although these ships do not look glamorous, they are one of the most urgently needed and most vital cogs in our offensive defense of this country." Company managers paid tribute to the workers and department heads. Charles Pillsbury, general manager of the CBI shipbuilding program, noted "A year ago last Tuesday, the first keel was laid. At that time, there was only a small beginning. The shipyard, as you see it today, is a testimonial to the foresight of our own engineers . . . and the skill of the subcontractors who constructed the facilities."

That same day, LST 212 was christened by Katherine Trees. US Navy photo.

While the Navy was being hosted at Seneca, Peru was planning for the arrival of hundreds of army personnel from the 740th MP battalion from Camp Skokie in Glenview; the 732nd MP battalion from Camp Des Plaines near Joliet; and the 20th Armored Division from Camp Campbell, KY. The men had an exhibition at Kewanee on June 10 and were coming to LaSalle-Peru on June 14.

At about 9 a.m., they set up camp at the Pulaski Street show grounds. The soldiers brought a variety of military weapons and other pieces of equipment. The display was set up in LaSalle at Second and Hennepin.

Some of the armor on display included a General Grant tank (above) and a Stuart tank (left).

The army also brought a 33-ton Sherman tank to display in LaSalle. Other weapons included a 105mm howitzer, a 37mm anti-tank gun and a 40mm Bofors anti-aircraft gun.

Some of the less lethal pieces of equipment included a field ambulance, a 17-ton wrecker, an amphibious jeep, and a Link trainer. The flight simulator was developed by Edwin A. Link in the 1930's and initially marketed to amusement parks with few takers. The Army Air Corps bought six of the Model 6271 trainers. Ironically, the Japanese government also bought some of the trainers before the war.

Link trainers were commonly used to familiarize pilots with the typical controls they would find in many of the navy and army air force planes.

Left: In 2005, one of the original Link trainers was under restoration at the Western Museum of Flight in Hawthorne, CA. It is painted in the traditional Army Air Force colors with a blue fuselage and yellow wings, elevator, and rudder.

During the day, about 200 of the soldiers were taken on tours of the local industries including Westclox, Carus Chemical, M&H Zinc, Illinois Zinc, Mineral Point Zinc, American Nickeloid, the Marquette, Lehigh, and Alpha cement companies, Eicor, Sampsel Time Controls, the Maze nail factory, the Union and Osage coal mines, Illinois Machine Tool, Chamberlain Weather Stripping, H.D. Conkey Engineering, and Star Union Brewery.

The *Post-Tribune* reported that some of the local soldiers involved in the event were Sgt. Stan Grubich (LaSalle), Pfc Howard Sibigtroth (Peru), Pfc John Talauskas (Oglesby), Jim Ceressal (Spring Valley), and Pvt. Dominic Barton (Seatonville).

On Monday evening at 6 p.m., a parade was led by a 40-piece band from the 740th battalion. The floats, representing the Red Cross, Boy Scouts, unions, and civic organizations, started at

Sixth and Pulaski in Peru and followed a route south to East Fifth Street and east to Joliet Street and headed to Third Street in LaSalle. The marchers then turned west to Bucklin Street, and disbanded at Fifth Street.

One of the parade units represented the Green River Ordnance Plant. The traveling museum had a display of the artillery shell components and empty shells that normally would be filled with explosives manufactured at the plant.

In the evening, a program was held at the L-P practice football field. It began with one of the sergeants demonstrating how a pup tent could be set up in just a few minutes. That was followed by an exhibition of precision drill by a platoon from the 740th MP and another unit from the 732nd battalion.

The climax of the army show was a mock battle staged by 70 men of the 740th battalion. Officers in charge of the event decided against using their tanks and anti-tank guns, which would have ripped up the sod. Preparations for the show had been made by pre-positioning "land mines," which consisted of half-pound cans of TNT, the same type of charge used in actual training. They would be electronically detonated during the "attack."

The "battle" began with a series of explosions from aerial bombs. Snipers on one side engaged the scouts of the opposition. Casualties were removed by stretcher bearers while rifle fire and machine gun bursts, coupled with exploding land mines and mortar rounds, simulated by aerial explosions, filled the night air with the acrid odor of gunpowder. The *Post-Tribune* reported the next day, "It took little imagination to picture an actual battlefield. The only thing lacking was the sight of blood."

The following day, June 15, the huge army show moved to Ottawa. The soldiers set up their camp at the Fairgrounds Park on Route 6. The Ottawa *Daily Republican* characterized it as an "invasion" by a thousand men and their military equipment. The army tribute to agriculture, labor, and industries in LaSalle County included exhibits set up at the end of LaSalle Street and in the municipal parking lot. It was the first time for many residents to see the weapons being used in the war. The soldiers spent the day explaining the operation of various small arms, the .30 caliber Garand rifle, machine guns, and mortars. Other equipment on display included a 37mm anti-tank gun, a 105mm howitzer, and a 40mm Bofors anti-aircraft gun. The new five-man Sherman tank with its 75mm cannon was of special interest. Altogether there were 125 different pieces of motorized equipment on display.

Weapons on display included a 105mm howitzer and a Sherman tank.

That evening at 6:15 p.m., a parade of army units and civic groups passed the reviewing stand in Washington Park. Following the parade, a program was held in the east section of the Fairgrounds. Another mock battle was acted out by the military units before an audience of as many as 12,000 spectators.

It was back to routine work the following day. R.C. Carter and John Walter, who headed the Mendota Salvage drive, reported that the scrap drive was going well in June. The collection of the scrap was made possible in part due to the use of trucks provided by Mr. Lambert Jones and the Fahler Oil Co. Drop off points included the Alexander Lumber Co. and the Fahler Motor Co. A separate collection point for tin cans was set up near the Central Oil Station. All of the money received for the scrap was donated to the Boy and Girl Scouts, the Red Cross, and the Civilian Defense organization. The committee also publicly thanked the Rapp Repair Shop, Roy Williams, Claude Watson, Amelia Walter, Ella Gesslein, and Miss Dennison for their contributions to the salvage effort in Mendota.

In early July, attention turned to the approaching canning season. Food for troops and civilians alike was dependant on a good harvest and the subsequent processing of the vegetables. Since the war started, Mendota faced a shortage of workers to process vegetables. The increased wartime demand resulted in farmers planting more crops, so the Inderrieden canning factory started recruiting older men, women, and younger teenagers – everyone else it seemed was working in war plants or in the service. The company even planned on a four-hour evening shift so that workers with day jobs could also work a part time shift at the cannery. When the pea crop was ready at Hampshire, IL, it was necessary for the Mendota Canning Co. to send workers to that location to help with the canning after they had already put in a full day in Mendota. The work continued into the night when soldiers from Camp Grant were brought in as a relief force. Cannery managers could only hope that there would be enough workers available in the weeks ahead to avoid that situation in the Mendota area.

Illinois Valley residents were constantly exposed to information about both the progress and the setbacks of the war. The local press tended to stress the positive stories, such as the massive bombing raid by B-25's over Sicily and the first downing of a Focke-Wulf 190 by an African-American pilot in a P-40 Warhawk, which was escorting the Mitchell bombers. Readers also noted the front page story of the Independence Day dedication of the new Electrical Utilities Co. on North St. Vincent Street in LaSalle. Descriptions of progress on the factory had been in the local papers for months, and finally, on July 5, the factory was about to begin the production of a variety of electrical condensers. These were essential components for timing devices, control equipment, telephones, broadcast transmitters and receivers, and the new "top secret" radar.

While such events commanded front page coverage, smaller efforts to win the war were not overlooked. As part of their "Retailers For Victory" campaign, the Tri-City merchants adopted the motto, "Bomb Tokyo With Your Small Change" that same week. They hoped to raise $26,000 worth of bonds and war stamps. The fund-raising effort was part of the nationwide campaign to finance the new aircraft carrier *USS Shangri-La* whose task it would be to launch an attack on Tokyo and avenge the attack on Pearl Harbor. The retailers in LaSalle, Peru, and Oglesby even offered monetary prizes to the newspaper boys who sold the most war stamps.

Tri-City shoe stores were suffering from slow sales due to the rationing system. Fortunately, there was a short period of relief, July 19-July 31, when OPA had authorized stores to have a special sale for slow-moving and odd-lot shoes without the normal requirement for a shoe ration stamp. To ensure that this would not generate a wholesale reduction of any and all shoes that retailers deemed "slow-movers," OPA specified that no more than 1 to 4 percent of a retailer's inventory could be so classified. Maybe the relaxation of the shoe rationing was to soften the blow coming in August for motorists. The entire Midwest was facing a 25 percent reduction in gasoline supplies. Beginning at midnight on Sunday, Aug. 15, the "A," "B," and "C" gas coupons that had allowed drivers to purchase four gallons would only allow service station attendants to pump three gallons. The maximum allowance for work-related driving was slashed from 720 miles per month to 480 miles. The only persons exempted were doctors, ministers, and certain workers in war industries.

When *Post-Tribune* readers were drawn to a July 20 article titled "Navy 'Cruiser' Here Wednesday and Thursday," they quickly learned that it wasn't really the naval ship that they might have expected. The "cruiser" turned out to be Navy recruiting trailer that was "docked" in front of the LaSalle National Bank. The Navy personnel on hand were not only recruiting potential sailors and WAVES but also seeking men, 17-50 years old, who had construction skills needed by the Seabees.

Although German bombers had never reached New York, let alone the Illinois Valley, civil defense authorities in Illinois (with the exception of the Chicago metropolitan area) decided to schedule another air raid blackout at the end of July. The blackout the previous summer had been carried out without serious flaws, so civil defense committees throughout the Illinois Valley hoped that the 1943 blackout would eliminate any violations.

Once again, there were weeks of planning by local civil defense organizations, police, fire departments, volunteer organizations, such as the American Legion, and the military. In

Ottawa, Charles McClellan, the Ottawa civil defense coordinator, said that the city would fire three aerial bombs to indicate the beginning of the blackout. Another aerial bomb would signal the "all clear" termination of the exercise. The July 30 drill would only last ten minutes at most and followed the pattern established in 1942. Talking to a reporter from the *Republican Times*, McClellan said, "We had an excellent record in the previous blackout. Relatively few lights were noted in business places and homes. We hope that tonight here there will be absolutely no violations." He explained that pedestrians were expected to take cover and remain off the streets. Flashlights would be banned and as would the lighting of cigarettes. The only exception to the blackout regulations would be at the Seneca shipyard. Walter Colby, director of public relations at the shipyard, stated that floodlights and other illumination for the night crew would not be extinguished because "it would slow up production."

Two squads from the Illinois Reserve Militia, Company E from Ottawa were assigned to assist the warden in Marseilles. In addition, a number of Marseilles Legionnaires were sworn in to act as special police. Everyone seemed to be prepared for the following night's blackout.

On July 30 in the Tri-Cities, a five-minute period of shrieking sirens and whistles preceded the 9:40 p.m. blackout. Local post offices participated for five minutes, and factories turned out their lights for two minutes. The test in the Tri-Cities was deemed highly successful. Motorists complied everywhere by pulling off to the side of the road and extinguishing their headlights. Initially, there was some confusion when the bell in one Spring Valley church was rung prematurely. *(Note – a Spring Valley request for a siren had been denied by the WPB.)* Drivers from Peru traveling west on Route 6 to Spring Valley after the "all-clear," ran into a small traffic jam at Webster Park where drivers had dutifully stopped but, not hearing another signal, had not resumed their travel when the drill ended.

In Oglesby, Mayor John Pryde expressed his satisfaction with the community's response. Civil Defense Coordinator Joseph Caveletto also expressed his appreciation for a job well done by his civil defense workers.

There were mixed results in Ottawa, where the state militia reserve was on patrol with car headlights covered in red cellophane as they checked for violations. McClellan conceded that the blackout was not 100 percent successful. One driver refused to cooperate when ordered by an air raid warden to pull over. His license plate number was recorded and sent to the control center. The L-O-F plant, where workers were on the night shift making airplane canopies, cooperated by turning off the lights for only five minutes, as was requested by the defense council, but failed to extinguish two floodlights in the parking lot. Several businesses failed to extinguish all of their lights. A neon light was on in one business in the 200 block of West Madison. Other lights were still on at a gas station north of the Rock Island tracks, a garage on Madison, and two stores on LaSalle Street.

Virgil Outman, the secretary of the Marseilles council of defense, reported that almost the entire city was blacked out within two minutes of the start of the exercise. He said, "Watchers at the National Biscuit eight-story building, who were able to view Marseilles and the entire countryside, reported that the blackout was almost 100 percent perfect. Enemy planes would have found it difficult to detect a target in this area." He credited Dan Becker, the chief air raid warden, and his assistant, Andrew Buffo, with the success of the drill.

Civilians could take pride in their participation and cooperation with local authorities in such exercises. They could also be proud of the men they were supporting overseas. Periodically, the local newspapers ran front page stories of local servicemen who had distinguished themselves in battle. One of those men from LaSalle was Army Pvt. Robert Newton, son of Mr. and Mrs. Abraham Newton. In August 1943, a message finally reached LaSalle that Newton had been awarded the Soldier's Medal (at right) for heroism at a seaplane base in the Solomon Islands on Feb. 22. Although the soldier was  not connected with the naval detachment that came under aerial bombardment, Newton, a former L-P athlete, distinguished himself by ignoring explosions at the ammunition dump, and rushed through the flames to administer first aid to wounded sailors thus saving several lives. Newton's bravery was just one example of the hundreds of men from the Illinois Valley who received medals for their heroism.

Cities in the Illinois Valley became accustomed to inviting military heroes and noted civilian celebrities to speak at community luncheons and war production plants. One of those special guests was Mrs. Jimmie Doolittle, who was making a series of stops at war production plants. On Aug. 3, 1943, Mrs. Doolittle got off the Santa Fe train at Streator, where she was met by a delegation of workers from Owens-Illinois Glass, who escorted her to the plant for an inspection tour.

Mrs. Doolittle was greeted by Isabelle Butterfield when she arrived in Streator to visit the Owens-Illinois glass plant. *Line O' Nine*, Aug. 13, 1943 edition.

The *Line O'Nine* Owens-Illinois newspaper on Aug. 13 described her visit. Speaking to the workers, she stressed the importance of every worker doing his or her utmost to help bring an end to the war. She said, "Keep busy – as busy as you can – and then find some more to do. Participate in war work, either voluntarily or remunerative, to the limit of your ability. Blood donations, bond buying, watchfulness against carelessness and overconfidence will help save lives and end the war. Continue the good work on the home front."

It took more money than anyone could have foreseen to make America into an "Arsenal of Democracy." So, officials in Washington promoted the Third War Loan Drive, which started September 9. Within a week, Putnam County Banks were reporting success in meeting the established quotas. The Granville National Bank reported receipts of over $20,000 without even counting rural sales. $53,000 of the $56,000 quota for McNabb-Magnolia had already been subscribed.

Jeanne Hart was featured in the Owens-Illinois *Line O' Nine* newspaper on Oct. 1, 1943 promoting the purchasing of bonds in the Third War Loan Bond Drive. As of Sept. 30, the Streator "OnInzers" purchased bonds totaling more than $19,000.

Headlines described the bank reports of successful bond sales; the exuberance of young children going door to door collecting scrap metal; and celebrations of more ship launchings at Seneca. The stories about individual servicemen still had the greatest impact on families.

Western Union telegrams often meant that a serviceman was missing or had been killed, but in some cases, the information they carried could be hopeful. Such was the case for Mrs. Tomasa George, mother of Pvt. Joseph Lopez of DePue. First, he was reported to have been captured. Later, a second message said that he was in a POW camp in southern Germany. The Red Cross wrote telling Mrs. George that she would soon have his address.

Another soldier, who was taken prisoner by the Germans, was Tech Sgt. Ben Borostowski. The serviceman from LaSalle was a radio operator and gunner on a B-17 when it was believed to have been shot down while on a bombing mission over the Focke-Wolfe aircraft factory at Bremen, Germany. Although he was first reported missing in action on April 17, Borostowski was able to send his mother a letter from the prison camp by way of the German Red Cross. On June 16, the *Daily Post* printed his letter on the front page. In part, the letter read, "I'm allowed but two  letters and four cards a month. My greatest requirement is a warm cap of some sort and warm underclothing. I wish you could send me a pair of shoes. Also if possible try to get a heavy blanket for me." The Germans only allowed prisoners to receive one 11-pound parcel every 60 days. However, there were fewer restrictions on the number of letters prisoners could receive.

After seeing the letter in the newspaper, a number of service station operators, meeting with the ration board at the Hotel Kaskaskia, responded by taking up a collection, which amounted to $8.30, enough for that pair of shoes. A special ration certificate had to be issued to permit his mother to buy the shoes. After the meeting, seven of the men even offered to donate their No. 18 shoe coupon from their ration books if Mrs. Borostowski had used her coupon.

The Japanese also filled their POW camps from the earliest days of the war. One of those captured in the fighting at Corregidor in the Philippines was Marine Cpl. John Negro of Ladd. First reported missing on May 11, 1942, his parents finally received notification in July that he was in one of the Japanese POW camps. His mother, Mary Negro, was one of the thousands of workers at the Green River Ordnance Plant. A fellow worker at the plant, Mae Bovee of Oglesby, also learned that her husband, Capt. Frank W. Bovee, was a POW in the Philippines. When she was asked about her husband's captivity she said. "I wish the boys over there could know what's being done here. There wasn't enough ammunition on Corregidor to defend it. Every projectile I see go out of here I'm wishing Frank would have had it." The parents of Clayton Rundle of Oglesby received similar news. Their son was also in a Japanese POW camp somewhere around Manila Bay. Nothing was said about the physical condition of either serviceman. The Japanese Red Cross was handling letters and packages for the prisoners.

Another sailor held as a POW was seaman Abe Jacobs of Ottawa. His mother, Florence M. Jacobs, had not heard a word about her 20 year old son until she received a navy telegram on

Mar. 10, 1943. Finally, on Aug. 13, she received a card from the Japanese stating that he was at POW camp No. 3 in the Philippines. Jacobs indicated on the card that he was uninjured, in fair health, and he expressed hope that he would be home soon.

Individuals and groups tried to supply POW's with care packages whenever possible. There were also requests for personal items from a variety of concerned groups. The Friends of Service Men (FOSM) based in San Francisco started a "Hair Clippers For Heroes" campaign. The appeal, which went out to every American Legion post, explained that the old fashioned hair clippers were especially needed by surgeons who needed to quickly clip the body hair around wounds. The need was less urgent but also important for the ordinary soldiers in the Solomons and Africa who, in many cases, did not have time to shave but used the clippers to occasionally trim their beards. The LaSalle-Peru American Legion Post responded with enthusiasm, and within days, had more than a dozen clippers ready to be shipped.

Even a card from a POW camp was encouraging for worried friends and relatives. Front page news about two Mendota servicemen was more tragic. Sgt. Frank Conavit, a former resident, was killed when his plane crashed near McDill Field, Tampa, FL. Mrs. Josephine Coss of 1005 Monroe Street also feared the worst when she received a telegram saying her son, Staff Sgt. Bernard Coss, 19, had bailed out of their bomber while over the jungles of Dutch Guiana on April 9. On May 30, his death was confirmed by the War Department.

There were also stories of a more positive nature. One piece of good news for the Rev. W.Z. Dial in Mendota was that his son, Staff Sgt. I.W. Dial, not only had been promoted to 2nd Lieutenant. but was also awarded both the Air Medal and the Distinguished Flying Cross. The Mendota H.S. graduate had earned his wings in July 1942 and had flown 50 missions over New Guinea operating the "Bully Deed Express."

The blue and red Air Medal (at left) and the blue and orange Distinguished Flying Cross (at right) were awarded for meritorious air service.

Putnam County families also felt the uncertainties and anxiety connected with war. It wasn't until the end of September 1943 that Mrs. Ruth Forney of Granville learned that her son, Staff Sgt. Norman Forney, was missing in action and presumably shot down over Europe. Forney had served as a radio man and tail gunner on a bomber. In October, she was informed that her son was a prisoner of war. It would not be until February 1944 that Mrs. Forney, accepted the Air Medal for her son's "meritorious achievement." Fortunately, Sgt. Forney was able to survive the  ordeal of the prison camp, and the Germans allowed him to write home on a regular basis. When Germany was finally liberated in 1945, Forney was set free, and he returned to Putnam County.

Unfortunately, many medals were awarded posthumously. Ladd suffered its first casualty when Sgt. Harold E. Russell was killed while flying a mission over the Mediterranean. Russell was a tail gunner on a B-25, which was reported as missing in action.

A B-25 Mitchell bomber flies over the Mediterranean. Sgt. Russell was remembered for his sacrifice by fellow veterans after the war in the naming of the Ladd American Legion Post. *History of Ladd American Legion Post*, Nov. 1986.

Examples of personal hardships and tragedies were especially hard to accept, not only for the individual family, but also for everyone in the smaller towns. Another name was typically posted to the memorial honor roll of those who had sacrificed their lives, and life went on.

The need for both "guns and butter" required a continued concern for both aspects of home front production. Victory gardens made a significant difference in the availability of food in the summer of 1943. The federal government took over local canneries so that local growers could bring their produce to the canneries for processing. A.I. Fleming of Princeton, the supervisor of the Woolley Gardens Canning Center in Dover said, "People of the Bureau County community are appreciating this service offered at the Dover plant and are co-operating very well." Fleming asked Bureau County growers to bring in their harvests as early in the morning as possible to avoid overtaxing the capacity of the plant. Over 21,000 cans were put up in July alone. Corn and peas were processed every Monday, Wednesday, and Friday. Other vegetables were canned on Tuesdays and Thursdays. Classes were even offered for those who wanted to learn the canning process at seven Princeton churches or one of the home centers in Princeton operated by Mrs. Fred Alleri, Mrs. John Crist, Mrs. Hannah Grampp, Mrs. Franz Simon, and Mrs. Park Stratton.

Because of the shortage of agricultural workers, the federal government supported the importation of Caribbean islanders with temporary passports, who were hired to work throughout the entire Midwest. Pioneer Seed Co. brought in about 90 Jamaicans to detassel 900 acres of seed corn owned by the company in Bureau County. Before being transferred to Bureau County, the islanders had been helping at a cannery at Lenark in Carroll County. Pioneer had also hired 150 Jamaicans for their plant at Rochelle. Employers in Lenark and Rochelle reported that the Jamaicans were well-behaved, polite, and religious. Many were married with families on their island. The first 41 Jamaicans were to arrive in the Princeton area on July 24. Another 50 workers would arrive the following week. They were housed at the Bureau County Fair Grounds until the job was finished in mid-August. While in the fields, the Jamaicans would work in separate fields from other Bureau County employees, but they would be in Princeton from time to time and were not confined to the fair grounds. The Rev. Leslie Matson of the First Christian Church had spent ten years in Jamaica and invited the workers to join in Sunday services. Officials at Pioneer Seed Co. emphasized the fact that they still needed 150-200 workers from Bureau County to complete detasseling.

One new crop planted by many farmers in the Illinois Valley was hemp. Those who signed contracts with the federal government to grow this crop were frustrated by the wet weather that had delayed much of the planting. But by mid-June, about 75 percent of the seeding was completed. They looked forward to their first hemp harvest in late August. In the meantime, an office was opened in the Knauf Building in Ladd while the mill was under construction. Elmer Flaherty was appointed manager with R.S. Dailey as his assistant. The Ladd hemp territory extended from Manlius Township on the west to Waltham Township in LaSalle County on the east and from LaMoille on the north to Magnolia on the south. Other processing plants in the area were built at Wyoming and Earlville.

Farmers growing hemp were grouped into rings varying from 100 to 140 acres, each of which had one harvester and one binder. The farmers in each ring selected one man to operate the harvester. The rings were subdivided into five sections, each of which was supervised by a field man who helped maintain the machinery and generally assist in the harvesting process. The field men chosen for the area were Howard Sucher, Howard Baker, Bart Manning Jr., Pete Ternetti, and R.S. Dailey. Peter Hopkins and Ed Frey were hired as mechanics for the area.

Farmers in the Earlville area were informed that the harvesting equipment arrived on Aug. 5. They were to go to the Woods Implement Co. to receive instructions on the operation of a hemp binder. Wesley Kleinhas, the assistant manager of the hemp production, had joined the navy, so Pierre Meagher was called in from Decatur. During the following week, meetings were held at the farms of George Pratt, Will Pratt, A.P. Peterson, Norman Willard, Cal Hughes, H.L. Gletty, Rufus Butler, and Earl Moyer.

On Aug. 20, the hemp farmers were given a demonstration of the mechanical turners, which were built at the Tower Co. in Mendota. They met at the farm of Oscar Boltz, 1½ miles west of Earlville on Route 34. The new machinery was designed to alleviate the most tedious aspect of hemp production, the hand-turning of the sheaves. Engineers from War Hemp Industries were on hand to witness the demonstration and possibly approve the production of the equipment. After visiting the Boltz farm, E. P. Flickinger, manager of the Earlville hemp mill, and Fred Painter, LaSalle county farm advisor, led tours at the farms of Tillman and Kaminky, Herbert Gast, and J.W. O' Donnell.

In September, the hemp was cut with a special "hemp harvester." The retting process took an additional ten days to three weeks depending on the weather. Then, "gatherer-binder" machines were used to pick up the hemp and bind it into bundles, which were shocked. If the bundles were not shocked, and it rained, the hemp would rot on the ground.

The hemp plant in Ladd, IL, which was one of 11 in Illinois, was housed in these buildings photographed in 2005. After the war in 1949, the buildings were acquired by Illinois Industrial Rubber, a manufacturer of a variety of rubber products. Other manufacturers that occupied the building over the years included the Waukesha Rubber Co. and Parker Seals.

The *Putnam County Record* noted that Wilbur Sutherland was the first farmer in Putnam County to harvest the hemp plants on his farm southeast of McNabb. Another farmer in the McNabb area, Ellsworth Zellmer, recalled that in 1943, when he was 22 years old, he helped his father, William Zellmer, harvest the hemp on a 20-acre field they planted. Some of the stalks where so tall that they spilled over the edges of the trailer they used to haul the hemp to Ladd. Ellsworth said that he felt that a lot of the crops during the war were probably never processed since so much hemp was grown in the area.

While farmers had plenty of gas during the war, commuters, driving to war plants every day, had to be ever mindful of tire and gas rationing. This quickly stimulated an interest in car-pooling. The "Share–the–Ride" program caught on at Owens-Illinois Glass. Charlie Partridge of Cornell, IL, started driving the 30-mile round trip from Cornell to Streator with five co-workers from Cornell and another O-I worker from Streator.

They all worked in the packing department. Partridge was featured in O-I newspaper for his effort to save on gas and tires.

Owens-Illinois car-poolers:
Front center: John Hardin,
Center row: Charlie Partridge, Russell Sullivan, Ken Turner,
Back row: Farrell Gourley, Mary Muhlstadt, and Erma Meils.
Line O'Nine, 1943

In August 1943, new OPA regulations mandated changes in ride-sharing arrangements. If other members of the car pool had vehicles, they would have to rotate drivers so that no one driver would be able to save his "A" coupons, which allowed for about 150 miles of "pleasure" driving.

The OPA ration limits on beef may have been the reason behind an incident reported on a farm in Brookfield Township. The possibility of black marketers moving through the county and killing cattle made the front page of the *Republican Times* on July 30. John Madaus, who had a farm 4½ miles south of Marseilles, reported to Sheriff Clayton Harbeck that one of his calves had been killed, partially butchered, and covered with leaves and brush. He speculated that the perpetrator must have been scared off and planned to return to the scene later. Following the report, county officials issued a warning to residents not to buy black market meat, which might have been slaughtered under unsanitary conditions and could be very dangerous to eat. Fortunately, the supply of beef was improving, and limits were about to be eased. No other incidents were reported in the local press.

While stories of counterfeit ration coupons made the headlines in certain areas, the theft of coupons shocked readers of the LaSalle *Post-Tribune* on Aug. 27, 1943. The Tri-City rationing board kept a stockpile of extra coupons in its office safe. On Aug. 26, burglars stole the 400-pound safe with coupons that would allow the purchase of 200,000 gallons of gasoline. In addition, the safe contained 95,800 food coupons and certificates for 63 tires. Rather than try to open the safe on the premises, the thieves took the safe to the stone quarry east of LaSalle and broke off the combination lock with a heavy hammer. The safe was found the next morning by Walter Hasselman, an employee at the quarry. After the initial crime scene investigation, Deputy Sheriff Stan Murray concluded that the burglary involved at least three men. The investigation continued in the weeks that followed, but the perpetrators were not apprehended. The burglary had been one of several involving theft in ration board offices in Illinois. The LaSalle office was temporally closed until another safe and replacement ration books were obtained.

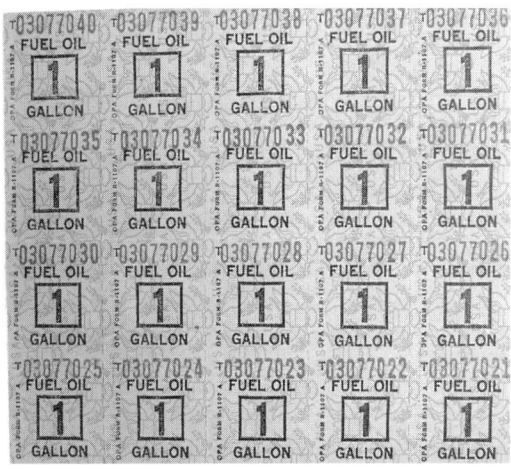

Fuel oil was also being rationed. Streatorland Historical Society.

To reflect changing farm production, OPA made frequent adjustments in the point system. A new listing of points for meat and dairy products was published in September 1943. One of the significant increases came for butter. It added two red points to the usual 10 points per pound. The rationale was the supply was continuing to decrease. However, OPA did decrease the points for 35 cuts of fresh meat, including lamb and mutton, bacon, pork, and beef ribs, roasts, and steaks. The supply of pork was up 13 percent over the August estimates, and the lamb supply had increased as well.

The blue ration stamps, used for canned goods, were also affected. Thirteen point values increased, but there were eight decreases. OPA explained that canned cranberries, peaches, apples, and pears were in short supply. The point value of canned beans, pumpkin, and squash was raised. Even dried prunes, raisins, and currants were added to the "rationed" list. OPA also reported, "The supply is still far below the buying demand." About the only bright spot in rationing was a relaxation in the points required for canned green and wax beans, and the large cans of tomatoes. That was explained by the current harvest of fresh vegetables, which was soon available in local stores.

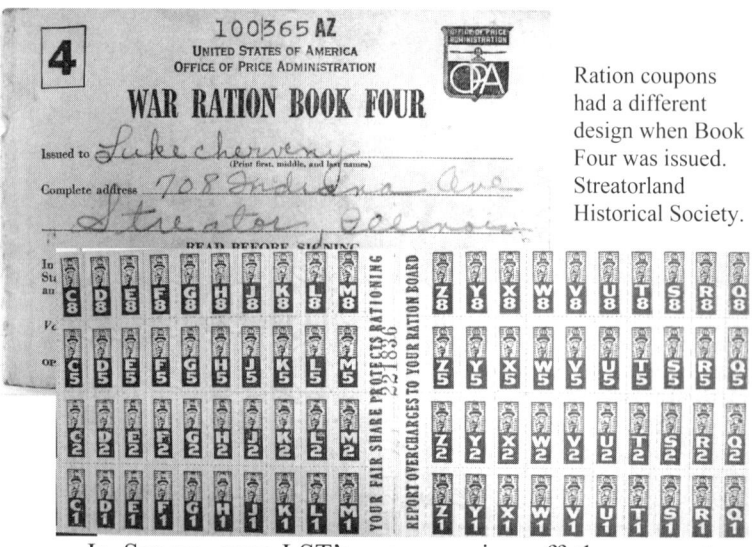

Ration coupons had a different design when Book Four was issued. Streatorland Historical Society.

In Seneca, new LST's were coming off the ways at an astounding rate. About once a week, another ship slid into the Illinois River. Ruth Clydesdale of Utica was selected to christen LST 222 on Aug. 17, 1943. Her husband was a carpenter at the yards, and her three sons, Robert, 22, William, 24, and Thomas, 25, were all in the armed forces. The ship launching was described in the paper as a "speed launching." The whole affair lasted about five minutes. A similar type of speedy launching was given to

LST 224 on Aug. 31. Gertrude Shoemaker of Ottawa, whose husband, Lt. George Shoemaker, was in charge of LST outfitting and the spare parts department, gave the hull a quick hit with a bottle of champagne, and the transport slid down the ways.

The woman who was chosen to christen an LST typically was a shipyard worker who had members of the family in the military. For example, Mary Oklesen, a 22 year old drill press operator, who was chosen for the honors on Sept. 7, had five brothers in the army. Rudolph was stationed in Fiji; Joseph and John were somewhere in Australia. The other two brothers, Edward and Vincent, were in North Africa. After Rev. F.W. Bruines, pastor of the Marseilles Congregational Church, gave the invocation, the Night Serenaders, a band made up of the Seneca night shift workers, played the national anthem. Then, Miss Oklesen simply said, "I christen thee LST 225," and cracked the bottle on the hull. Another LST was headed to the war.

Seneca workers were always anxious to see a returning veteran and listen to his experiences. On Sept. 1, 1943, while workers continued their welding and other jobs, the public address system broadcast an interview between Walter Colby and MM1c Sam Nauyalis from Spring Valley. It was the first time that a sailor who had crossed the ocean in an LST had visited the yard. During the invasion of Sicily, Nauyalis had survived the sinking of his ship when a German Messerschmitt made a direct hit.

After touring the engine room of one of the Seneca LST's, he was asked for his opinion of what he had seen. The young sailor commented, "Well, I think they are much better than many of the LST's I've seen, and I think the workers here take more care and pains and are doing a better job. As a whole, I think the ships, as far as I have seen down in the engine room, are very fine work."

His brother, Happy, who was a rigger on the LST's, took him around to meet other Spring Valley workers at the shipyard. Nauyalis said he was surprised by the number of ships under construction. He said to Colby, "I thought they were building one at a time at the river's edge instead of a huge yard like this." In his closing remarks, the Spring Valley sailor said to Colby, "I will tell you it takes several months from what I hear to build an LST, but I know from experience that it takes but a few seconds to sink one, so you see that's one reason why production should keep speeding up instead of cutting down. When you have broken a record for building a ship, try to break that record again on the next ship."

Over 10,000 workers were needed to produce the LST's, and there was a constant demand for workers. Ads for women, and girls and boys "over school age" appeared in the Ottawa newspaper. Salaries were good with union wages being paid. From those high wages the government called for contributions to the Third War Bond Drive. Ninety-seven percent of shipyard workers were already signed up for the payroll deduction plan. Nevertheless, CBI managers called for a two-day drive to reach their million dollar goal. The public address system boomed all day with messages encouraging workers to buy more bonds. The goal was to have every worker pledge the equivalent of two-week's pay for additional bonds. It seemed like a lot, but there was little doubt that the goal would be met.

Other towns responded to bond quotas set in proportion to their populations. Oglesby was given a goal of $125,000. To reach that level every man, woman, and child in Oglesby would have to spend $32 on bonds. Richard Moyle Sr., who was the chairman for the local drive, tried to get residents involved by having a Tuesday night community meeting at the Sacred Heart Church hall, where movies of actual battle scenes would be shown to inspire viewers. Films on the bombing of Tokyo and the battles of the Bismark Sea and Tunisia as well as the invasion of Sicily were to be shown. Pastor Theodore Wujek planned to make an appeal to his Sacred Heart congregation at the Sunday mass to attend the gathering on Tuesday night. Pastor Wujek said, "The drive is being speeded on by the realization that the combined efforts of everyone will be necessary in order that Oglesby's quota may be reached."

The Daughters of Isabella Society at Sacred Heart Church in Oglesby set up a booth at the Aida Theater during the following week and sold bonds totaling over $950. Other groups in Oglesby also got behind the drive. The American Legion Auxiliary headed by Mrs. Anna Prey and the Women's Club presided over by Mrs. Lewis Ebener also took their turn at the theater.

The bond drive committee in LaSalle tried a different approach. They planned to hold an auction rally at the corner of

First and Marquette Streets on Monday, Sept. 27, 1943. Donated merchandise would be auctioned off to bidders who paid for various items by purchasing the sale amount in bonds. To draw attention to the event, the Wilson Packing Company's six-horse team of Clydesdales was coming to LaSalle to pull the bond wagon. The committee also planned to include interviews with parents who had five sons in the service. Some of the mothers, who were asked to attend were Mrs. Silvester Kramarsic, Mrs. Bernardo Gerace, and Mrs. Anton Oklesen. Another special guest was Coxswain Frank Rady, who was home on furlough after having been in 11 naval battles.

On the day of the auction, The L-P High School band, directed by Lee Petersen, participated in a parade. The band marched to the Travis used-car garage at Second and Wright, where the Clydesdales were stabled. The parade participants marched to Joliet Street and finally ended up at the bank for the auction, where Clarence Elliott was the master of ceremonies.

The event was a great success bringing purchases of bonds with a maturity value of over $52,000. The top bidder was the local J.C. Penny store, which paid $8,000 for a miniature bar set and then promptly returned the set for another sale. Alex Hecht bought $4,000 in bonds for an American flag. Stuart Duncan was the high bidder with an offer of $2,000 for a box of shotgun shells.

Sunday, Sept. 26 marked another special event in Oglesby. Eicor officials formally accepted the $60,000 deed to their Oglesby plant since they fulfilled their promise to pay a million dollars in salaries. The Eicor workers contributed to the war effort by turning out motors, generators, and dynamotors, which were mainly used in military aircraft.

Although small towns lacked major industries like Eicor, they still did their bit to win the war. In Toluca, scrap drives were advertised in the Toluca *Star Herald*.

One of the regular features in the paper was "Company 'Ten . . . Shun'." It was a written by Audrey Maack, who corresponded with many of the servicemen. Her column included some of the soldiers' correspondence and other news about the servicemen and their families.

The Third War Bond Drive was just one of several fund raising activities. Another campaign in October was begun to raise money for the National War Fund. Donations to this fund were to be divided among seventeen agencies, the biggest of which was the United Service Organization (USO). Stuart Duncan was selected as the chairman for the LaSalle Community War Chest. A ten-day campaign to collect an average of $1 from every resident was established from Oct. 20 to Oct. 30. LaSalle Township's goal was $17,000. Even before the official start of the campaign, $4,000 was collected in LaSalle.

Illinois Governor Dwight Green and other civic and military officials promoted the war chest by marching in a rally in Ottawa on Friday, Oct. 16. When the march ended at Washington Park, Gov. Green spoke about the importance of the National War Fund and the local community chest. He expressed his appreciation to the people of LaSalle County, who had contributed $1.2 million in war bonds – almost twice as much as the previous year. He also called for the recruitment of more WACS and pointed to the need for another 1.24 million tons of scrap metal. The goal for the war chest was $34,522 in donations. When the campaign officially started on Monday, a local contractor, Gust E. Smith, made the first donation of $100.

In October 1943, Putnam County responded to the call from the governor to collect more scrap metal. Lawrence Ellena took on the responsibilities for organizing a scrap drive. November 12 and 13 were designated "round-up days" to collect scrap iron, tin, and paper. Tin was added to the list of essential metals because it was used to manufacture morphine-filled hypodermic syringes called syrettes. These were manufactured from almost 100 percent pure tin. Because the Japanese were in control of about 90 percent of all the tin-exporting areas previously used by the United States, it was essential to recycle tin cans. The tin found in two typical cans would be enough to make one syrette. Ellena said that in Putnam County the effort would be called the "Tin Can Drive." He called upon all of the students to remove the labels and bring clean, flattened cans to school.

Another type of collection drive was underway in Streator. Owens-Illinois employees took on the responsibility of making sure that fellow workers who had been called to duty would not be forgotten at Christmas. They started packaging gifts for 380 servicemen and women in mid-October 1943 to make sure they would arrive by Dec. 25. *Line O' Nine,* O-I newspaper, Oct. 28, 1943.

Not wanting to forget their co-workers, Westclox employees also sent holiday gift packages to former employees who had joined the armed forces. Volunteers packed each Christmas parcel with candy, sun glasses, books, uniform buttons, playing cards, and a Christmas card signed by D.J. Hawthorne, the general manager. They also packed V-mail stationary so the men could write home and three handkerchiefs – khaki-colored for the soldiers or white ones for the sailors.

Another group that supported the troops was the Bowlers Victory Legion. Stanley Selasek was selected to chair the association of 14 leagues that included the Westclox and the St. Joseph leagues. Donations from each team were used to purchase playing cards and pocket games for the troops. It was actually part of a nationwide campaign. By the end of the season, Illinois Valley bowlers had collected $412.

Two Hall H.S. alumni, who were killed while in the service, were remembered in a special way by the student body during an Armistice Day ceremony in 1943. Lt. Eugene Kuhre was killed in a plane crash, and Pfc. Arthur McNally, a paratrooper, died in Sicily. A program was held in the auditorium to honor them on Nov. 11. Following the assembly program, organized by Student Council President Norma Braida, two, six-foot Norway spruce tress were planted on the west side of the campus as a living memorial to their sacrifice.

On Oct. 24, 1943, the Green River Ordnance Plant held an Open House as a recruitment day. Musical entertainment was provided by soldiers from Camp Grant, Camp Ellis, and the Savanna Ordnance Plant. Sterling H.S. and Amboy H.S. also brought bands. Military equipment, including a Sherman tank, artillery pieces, and armored vehicles from the Rock Island Arsenal and the Savanna Ordnance Plant, were on display. Two of the lines at GROP were open, but cameras were forbidden. Paulsen, 21.

Over 25,000 visitors were able to see that safety measures were in place, and it was not as dangerous a place to work as rumors would have it. In fact, there was only one fatality which occurred when a rifle grenade exploded. Only dummy ammunition was displayed. However, this openness led to more job seekers. By the end of the year, over 4,500 employees – about half men and half women – were on the job. Paulson, pp 13-14.

Other ceremonies honored the workers at war production plants. The Army-Navy "E" pennants were not awarded to every factory. However, one company in Mendota that was recognized for its achievements was Conco Engineering Co. The business had war contracts for materials handling equipment, draft controls, and

Blitz cans for the government. Nov. 18 was selected for the presentation of the coveted "E" pennant to the company. "E" pins, along with engraved certificates, were also handed to every employee who made the award possible.

Thousands of servicemen traveling from Chicago to California often traveled by way of the Santa Fe Railroad. Although the troop trains stopped in Streator, there was only a small restaurant available for the men and women to order a quick meal or cup of coffee. Only a few could be served before the train pulled out of the station. One group of Streatorites came up with the idea of organizing a free canteen at the depot to alleviate the problem. The local Santa Fe agent, J.C. Murray, said that the group could use the depot. Several people said the idea was fine, but predicted that the effort couldn't be sustained for more than a month. Those doubters had no idea of the tenacity and dedication of Mary Plimmer and several other ladies from Streator who went ahead and decided to organize the Parents Service Club, which founded the Streator Free Canteen. Some of the other organizers were Mrs. Ray Eutsey, Mrs. Herman Beckendorf, Mrs. Charles Devine, Mrs. Josephine Dominic and Mrs. Joseph Harrison. Frank Behrens served as club president.

Canteen organizers Minnie Shull, Mary Plimmer, and Louise Mueller stand next to a service canteen cart donated by Thiedohr Drug Store in Streator.

Streatorland Historical Society.

They opened for the first time at 5 a.m., on Sunday, Nov. 28, 1943. Ten ladies made cookies and brought coffee in thermos jugs. Due to a scarcity of cups, the women had gone to their neighbors asking for empty cottage cheese containers. A long wooden table was set up to make hundreds of sandwiches. That first morning, over 300 soldiers, who were headed to San Francisco, were able to get a bag filled with the cookies and sandwiches. Unfortunately, there were more hungry troops than the ladies expected, so they took up a collection to buy more food for the men coming through Streator the next day.

In a 2005 interview, Mary Plimmer's niece, Sister Ann Rena Shinkey of Streator, recalled how her aunt went home and carved up the family's Sunday roast for sandwich meat. She said, "The canteen was the heart of her life. She started it because her son, William Plimmer, was in the service, as was her favorite nephew, Richard Dominic, who was a Seabee. According to Sister Ann, her aunt "wanted to do something nice for the boys coming through Streator hoping that a similar kindness would be given to her own boy." The service was offered seven days a week, whenever the trains were coming through Streator. Although there were all kinds of fruits and vegetables offered to the hungry travelers, she said, the servicemen "loved the Illinois tomatoes."

The Fern Leaf Circle volunteers at the canteen. Streatorland Historical Society.

The effort snowballed. Merchants began making donations. Soon, the women had an ice box, coffeepots, and tables. Farmers in the Streator area donated tomatoes, apples, and pears as well as sides of beef and pork. The Santa Fe Railroad built a kitchen and provided the water and electricity in the station to help the volunteers. Sam Danhoff was chairman of a group that sponsored a tag day to raise money for the kitchen, which opened on July 21. The Parent's Service Club remained as the organizing element at the Streator Free Canteen as other groups volunteered to man the canteen. A few of the groups that offered their help were the War Mothers Club, the Ottawa Navy Mothers Club, the Streator Navy Mothers Club, the Margaret Roper Club, the Junior Women's Club, the Fern Leaf Circle, the Knights of Columbus Auxiliary, and the Delta Theta Tau Sorority.

While Streator was the railroad hub for trains carrying men and material, Seneca shipyard was the center of LST activity. Forty ships had been launched by Thanksgiving 1943. Seneca LST's were soon taking American troops and supplies to the battlefields of the Pacific and the European Theaters.

The wartime image of the Rosie the Riveter stereotype is reflected in these young women from Streator who worked as drill press operators at the Seneca shipyard in 1943. Pictured are F. Rice, M. Hill, N. Godwin, M. Zera, T. Hess, K. Giacomini, and M. Childers. Streatorland Historical Society.

LST 205 was christened by Doris Dehaven and launched on April 13, 1943. There were several launchings of LST's every month at Seneca. US Navy photo.

View of the Seneca shipyard showing how the LST's were in various stages of production. *Our Prairie Shipyard*.

Winch trucks pulled the LST's to the center ways. *Our Prairie Shipyard*.

It appeared that LST's were the only type of ships being produced, but on Dec. 1, 1943, with little fanfare, the YF-613 was launched. The ship, measuring 260' x 48' x 27', was designated as a covered lighter. According to the CBI article, it was the only ship built for the Navy in Seneca that wasn't originally designated as an LST.
Our Prairie Shipyard.

Once outfitted, the Seneca-built LST's were formally commissioned and loaded for war. This Seneca-built LST was headed to Cape Gloucester in New Britain. US Coast Guard photo.

LST 511 was launched Dec. 3, 1943. It was photographed being turned around in the Illinois River. It was one of the ships that took part in the D-Day invasion.
Our Prairie Shipyard, January 1944.

The shipyard workers had many talents besides construction or administrative skills. Some of the workers organized to perform a theatrical production called "The LST Minstrels." It included a cast of 50 workers including the male chorus of the electrical department. Some of the local people who were in the group were Ramona Simpson (Dalzell), Edith Ryan (LaSalle), Celia Chemelewski (Peru), Veronica Jakubek (Peru), and Milo Springborn (Oglesby). Performances were held in Seneca, Marseilles, Ottawa, Morris, and LaSalle during late November and early December.

While naval activities were the focus of attention at Seneca, the army opened a camp down river at Starved Rock State Park in December 1943. Gov. Greene had given permission to the commander of Camp Ellis to use part of the state park to train engineers in pontoon bridge construction in simulated combat conditions.

The first army units arrived at the park in early December and lived in tents while they constructed wooden hutments, each of which housed 6-8 men. Some of these structures were interconnected to form a mess hall and kitchen. The engineers brought pontoons and bridge building equipment to be used in the six-month training program. Plans called for the construction of a variety of bridges ranging from pneumatic float bridges with a $12\frac{1}{2}$-ton capacity to 25-ton capacity bridges with spans ranging from 200 to 400 feet extending from park property to Plum Island in the Illinois River. After bridges were built, they were disassembled so the next group of trainees could repeat the program. The number of engineers involved in the program ranged from 500-600 during each 2-3 week course.

With so many servicemen in the area, a search was immediately initiated to establish a servicemen's club in LaSalle. The plan was enthusiastically endorsed by Mayor Orr, but he promised that no teenage girls would be allowed in the club, and it would not become a hangout.

A suitable building was found at 431 First St., LaSalle, and furnishings were donated by Tri-City Furniture, Hummer Furniture, and Freedman Furniture. An operating schedule was established with the club being open from 6:30 p.m. to 11 p.m.

during the week and later hours on the weekend. Dances were scheduled, and a Red Cross canteen was set up at the club.

One of the local men involved with the training at Starved Rock was Pvt. Walter Benedict of LaSalle. His unit was the 2nd Battalion of the 1303rd Engineers, the first unit sent from Camp Ellis. *Post-Tribune* photo, Dec. 28, 1943.

An idea began circulating among residents in the Tri-Cities and Ottawa to extend holiday hospitality to the army engineers by sharing Christmas dinner. Invitations were sent to the LaSalle *Post-Tribune*, which was coordinating the effort. The response was overwhelming. Within two days, so many families offered to open their homes to the servicemen that the newspaper had to inform the community that there were more invitations offered than soldiers stationed at Starved Rock. It was decided to match families with servicemen based on the order in which the invitations were received. The plan called for a distribution of the families offering Christmas dinners equally between the Tri-Cities and Ottawa.

Upon hearing of the tremendous outpouring of goodwill, one officer said, "This certainly shows the fine spirit in which people of your community are receiving our boys. Had we known of the wonderful reception, we were to receive this week, we might have made plans to bring more soldiers here."

Community cooperation in the Tri-Cities also extended to the Victory Waste Paper campaign sponsored by the *Post-Tribune*. Ever since November, the government had been urging the nation to save paper. Large ads described the paper crisis in the war plants. Citizens were informed of the widespread need for additional paper products ranging from the millions of boxes of K and C-rations for the troops to the tons of paperboard used to package munitions. Even the home front need for recycled paper was stressed since many food containers had been converted from metal to cardboard. The seriousness of the shortage was emphasized by pointing out that 25 paper-consuming war plants were in danger of a complete shutdown because of the lack of packaging materials. Everyone was encouraged to save newspapers, magazines, cardboard boxes, paper bags, letters, boxes, envelopes, and advertising material. The Starved Rock area Boy Scouts took charge of the collection. Several trucks, two from the Ramenofsky junk yard, one from Sol Ramenofsky fruit store, one from the National Biscuit Co., and another from Yellow Cab, were donated for the collection drive. Locally, Arthur Vohs was the chairman of the civic service committee in the LaSalle district.

The Kaskaskia Hotel also got involved in the salvage program as part of the nationwide "Salvage All Four For Victory Campaign." William Hahne, manager of the Kaskaskia, was also the state chairman of the hotels' collection efforts. In addition to paper, the hotels were collecting fats, scrap metal, and tin.

On the official pick-up day, Dec. 29, approximately 60 Boy Scouts in LaSalle canvassed the city, working from 9 a.m. until 10 p.m. A total of 22 tons of waste paper was collected.

Home front spirits were raised in December with the reassuring news that one of Peru's bluejackets, Casimir Pytel, had survived a harrowing encounter. Six Junkers 88's attacked his bomber while on an anti-submarine mission over the Bay of Biscay off the coast of France. First reports to his mother, Celia Pytel, said that the naval aviation ordnanceman was "missing in action." It was later determined that the plane, riddled with German cannon fire, had crashed, but the crew managed to get into life rafts and survived at sea for two days before being rescued. Pytel, who was reported to have suffered a back injury, was later presented with the Air Medal by Admiral Stark.

On the other side of the globe, more encouraging news was reported about the son of Mr. and Mrs. Glenn Calhoun of Wenona. Second Lt. John C. Calhoun, a Wenona H.S. graduate, was one of the crew aboard a photo-reconnaissance plane assessing bomb damage on Balikpapan, Borneo. After taking the pictures, the pilot dropped his bombs on a nearby oil refining and storage area and then sank a Japanese 6000-ton merchant ship. During the attack, the plane came under fire from anti-aircraft guns and a flight of Japanese interceptors. The American crew shot down four of the planes during the air battle. Later, the Wenona flyer was presented with the Silver Star by Gen. George Kenney.

This Christmas letter, cleared by the army censor, was sent by Dale Keilty on Oct. 25, 1943 to the John Van Meter family in Tonica. Mail from servicemen overseas was a great boost to morale on the home front.

Below: John Shimkus of Granville was one of hundreds of workers at the Sampsel Time Control Co. in Spring Valley during WWII. Arthur Sampsel and the other company officials sent out these letters for Christmas 1943 to express their appreciation for the work of their employees.

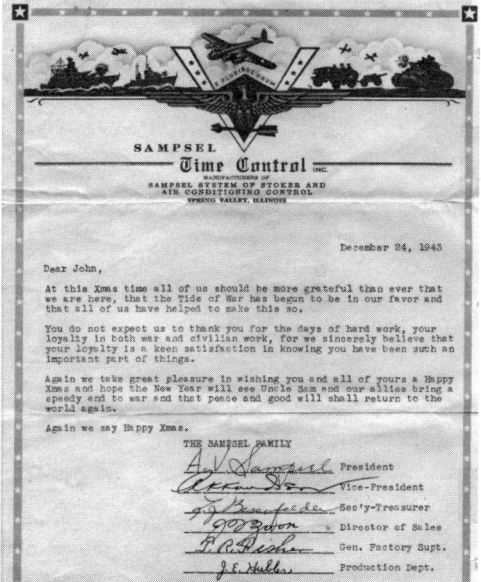

This WWII Christmas Card is also from the Shimkus collection.

CHAPTER FOUR
Turning The Tide

Local businesses, such as Moews Seed Co. in Granville, sponsored official government ads such as this one that appeared in a 1944 edition of the *Putnam County Record*.

On Jan. 11, 1944, many teenagers took a special interest in a *Post-Tribune* feature. What made the story unique was that Bill McNamara, the 14-year old son of Mr. and Mrs. Edward McNamara, had enlisted in the navy. The Ottawa H.S. freshman had convinced a navy recruiter that he was 17 by using a birth certificate from a brother, who had died in infancy. It wasn't until he was already in boot camp at Great Lakes that his chicanery was discovered by his parents, who contacted Sheriff Harbeck, who in turn contacted the naval authorities. His parents finally gave their written consent so that their teenage son could continue to serve his country. Bill was assigned to destroyer duty, and in less than a year, he was promoted to petty officer at age 15, perhaps making him the youngest petty officer in the U.S. Navy. The story may have been somewhat embarrassing to the navy, but it brought pride to one Ottawa family.

Attention shifted to the L-P High School auditorium on Jan. 25, when an awards program was held for Westclox employees. A letter addressed to the Westclox workers from Robert Petterson, Undersecretary of War, read in part, "The high and practical patriotism of you men and women of the Westclox division is inspiring. Your record will be difficult to surpass, yet the army and navy have every confidence that it was made only to be broken." General Manager D.J. Hawthorne was on the stage to accept the Army-Navy "E" pennant for outstanding achievement in the production of war materials. William Mauritzen, who had worked at Westclox since 1896, accepted "E" lapel pins on behalf of every member of the company.

During January, Companies A and B of the 1309th Engineers at Starved Rock grew more efficient in their bridge construction skills trying to improve on their time for construction and dismantling of a 25-ton, 340-foot pontoon bridge. The 1309th shaved 45 minutes off the best time of the 1306th Engineers, who had been encamped at the Rock two weeks earlier. The 74 men, many of whom were veterans of the fighting in the South Pacific, only needed 5 hours and 15 minutes to build the bridge to Plum Island. They also broke the record for dismantling the bridge by completing the job in 2 hours and 45 minutes. Their commander, Lt. Edward Dawson, told a *Post-Tribune* reporter, "The way these companies worked on the bridge was a sight to watch. Each man had a job to do, and it was carried out without a hitch."

While the engineers were stationed at Starved Rock, there was time for socializing with the local residents. Their 27-piece regimental band performed a concert at the corner of First and Wright Streets in LaSalle on Jan. 21. Later that same evening, 11 members of the band played for a servicemen's dance. Because almost the entire battalion was expected, the event was moved to the Auditorium, which the proprietor, "Tinney" Cosgrove, made available. Blanche Klein, the entertainment chairman, was in charge of the hostesses for the dances in LaSalle.

In addition to the dances, the soldiers were guests at a number of dinners sponsored by local organizations. A spaghetti supper was provided by the American Legion Auxiliary on Jan. 20. The Baptist churches in Utica, Oglesby, and LaSalle also took turns inviting groups of the engineers to dinners during February.

Recreational diversions for the men included swimming at the L-P High School pool and the Dickinson House in Oglesby. The commanding officer of the engineers said, "Swimming in the winter is truly a rare privilege seldom enjoyed by men in the army."

The servicemen's center in LaSalle was made a unit of the USO in early February so additional funds were provided by that organization. Otherwise, everything stayed pretty much the same. Mrs. Bradley Turner continued in her position organizing the volunteer help. Mrs. W.K. Hartshorn remained as the coordinator of Red Cross, which operated the food canteen, and Mrs. E.G. Marshall continued in her position as chairman of the house committee.

Because of the many services provided by the LaSalle servicemen's center during its daily schedule – especially the Monday and Friday dances – many women's clubs were asked to staff the canteen and provide refreshments, such as sandwiches, cakes, cookies, coffee, and soft drinks.

By the end of February, the special training program at Starved Rock was coming to an end. About 5,000 engineers had been at the state park over the course of the previous three months.

During the closing week of the encampment, Capt. William Dawson, the commander of the program, remarked to a reporter from the LaSalle *Daily Post-Tribune*, "The boys will turn from bridge builders to landscape artists." The grounds would be graded to remove the ruts caused by the heavy equipment, and the only visible sign of the encampment that would remain after the troops left would be the gravel roads built by the engineers.

On Mar. 1, a farewell dinner was held for the soldiers at Sacred Heart Church in Oglesby. The Daughters of Isabella served a spaghetti dinner to 125 men. Mrs. Maude Aimone, regent for the lady's group, had one group decorate the church hall in a patriotic motif featuring a replica of the Statue of Liberty, large American flags hung on two walls, and patriotic table decorations. At the dinner, the men applauded Richard Moyle Sr. for allowing them to use the facilities at Dickinson House. Following the after dinner speeches, Edward Urbanowski assisted in running films depicting the fighting at Tarawa as well as action in North Africa and Italy.

In February, the government had kicked off its fourth war bond drive. In order to display the new bond poster (right), it was necessary to oversubscribe previous bond pledges by at least $100.

One of the groups taking special interest in the drive were three wholesale liquor distributors, Consumers of LaSalle County, Bonucci Wholesale Liquor, and the Rinella Co. Herman Bonucci was the organizer for Bureau, Putnam, Henry, and Stark Counties. Joseph Campeggio took charge in LaSalle and Marshall Counties. David Dyke was the coordinator for Grundy, Lee, Livingston, and Kendall

Counties. Each of the 900 taverns in the region would try to sell $1000 in bonds. The goal was to finance three bombers at a cost of $300,000 each.

After the occupation of North Africa and invasion of Sicily, the Third Army was slugging it out with the Germans in Italy. To make headway against a stubborn enemy, a British-American invasion of Anzio was ordered. The allies scraped together 88 LST's, including LST 197, the first one launched at Seneca, to land the troops.

LST's landing in southern Italy. US Navy photo.

Aboard one of the landing craft in late February 1944 was Pfc. Harry A. Volant of Ladd (at right). While manning a heavy machine gun, his unit came under heavy attack from the Germans, and he was wounded in the eye with shell fragments. From his hospital bed in Italy, he was able to pen a short letter to his parents in Ladd letting them know that he was slightly wounded, and he would soon return to combat. Mr. Kerns, yard manager of Chicago, Milwaukee, and St. Paul RR at Ladd, received the message and took it to the Volant home. Surprisingly, the letter got to Ladd before the War Department notification arrived.

For his repeated acts of bravery, Volant, now decorated with the Purple Heart, was promoted to sergeant. After more months of fighting in southern France and Germany, Volant was finally discharged. Arriving at Camp Grant in Rockford, he spotted the caboose of a train and climbed abroad. Sitting inside was his father, Harry Volant Sr. His homecoming was a complete surprise.

The story was typical of many returning veterans. Generally, there were no grand parades or community receptions. Those celebrations would remain for the grand finale with the defeat of Japan.

Many male civilians in their late 30's and older, who had by virtue of their age thought they were safe from the draft call, might have been a little shocked to receive notification in late February that they were being reclassified. Generally, the local draft boards were not calling any men over 34, but now, all men under 38, even those with dependents, were being reclassified as 1-A unless they were in a war-essential industry. In addition, a new classification of 1-AH was assigned to men in the 38-45 age group. They did not have to worry about being called up unless the president raised the age limit.

Another new category, 4-AH, designated men 45-65. That group as well would not be called unless by Congressional edict. In any case, Frank Godawa, chief clerk of the Tri-City draft board, tried to put the older men as ease stating, "If you are over 38 years of age and get a 1-AH or 4-AH card from us in the next couple of days, don't telephone or come to our office seeking to know when you will be called, for the armed forces are not calling your class now and have no intentions of doing so."

OPA had decided back in October 1943 to introduce the use of ration tokens to make change for the 10-point paper stamps. The three-layered tokens, somewhat smaller than a dime, had either blue or red outer surfaces and a yellow inner layer, which was treated with a fluorescent dye to prevent counterfeiting.

It was not until February 16, that the *Post-Tribune* ran a front page article explaining how the tokens would be used as change effective Feb. 27. On that day, every old coupon would be valued at 10 points, and each new token would be worth 1 point. Each person would receive 50 blue-stamp points and 60 red-stamp points. If a shopping bill for canned fruits and vegetables required 25 points, the clerk would request 30 points in blue stamps and return 5 blue tokens for 5 points in change.

OPA was constantly issuing new point values for different products depending on the availability of a myriad of food items. At the end of January, the points for Swiss, Munster, and bleu cheese went up four points. Most beef cuts and pork loins went up slightly. The points for canned dried beef, beef tongue, pork, and Vienna sausage also increased. The only good news was that butter would remain at 16 points because of the increased supply.

By March, OPA was revising the points for juices and canned vegetables. Tomato juice, orange juice, and even grapefruit juice, which had not even been rationed for three months, were all going up in point value. Cans of apples, applesauce, peaches, pears, cherries, fruit cocktail, and pineapple would also require more points. Points for fresh lima beans and catsup went up too. However, due to outstanding participation in the victory garden program, the values of canned tomatoes, peas, and corn were going to be dropped substantially on Mar. 5. On the list of items not rationed were canned beans, dried prunes, raisins, currants, and mixed dried fruits.

The OPA was also charged with the responsibility of assuring the fair distribution of gasoline supplies and the maintenance of ceiling prices in restaurants. Because of a nationwide black market operation in counterfeit and stolen gas ration stamps by organized crime, the OPA district enforcement office in Peoria notified Illinois Valley gas station owners that inspectors would be posted at filling stations to examine motorists' ration books to see that they were properly endorsed.

Another change in store for drivers was a further decrease in the allotment for "A" gasoline coupons. Effective March 22, 1944, Midwest drivers could only purchase two gallons instead of three gallons a week for "pleasure driving." The East Coast states had already been cut to two gallons a week. OPA blamed the situation on decreasing fuel supplies. The only bright spot was that those car-pooling and holding "B" coupons would be allowed to appeal to their local boards for an additional allotment to make up for the reduction in the "A" coupon. Under the new regulations, "B" coupons were supposed to provide enough gas to drive 475 miles instead of 460 miles each month.

Inspections of LaSalle county restaurants were also scheduled for the first week of March. Copies of menus with listed prices from April 1943 had to be posted for inspection. This was to ensure that there had been no price increases during the previous year. Restauranteurs could not evade the regulation by simply cutting the traditional portions being served or dropping items from the meals to lower costs.

The average person might have thought that working in a munitions factory like the Green River Ordnance Plant near Amboy was extremely dangerous, and indeed, it was necessary to have stringent safety rules enforced at all time. They had a good safety record until Feb. 29, 1944, when there was an explosion on one of the shell-loading lines. As a result, Mrs. Edna Christy, a 38 year old widow from Princeton, was killed, and 11 other workers were injured. Among the Illinois Valley workers wounded by shrapnel were Russell Dhamers (Princeton), Juanita Baratta (Mendota), Doris Davis (Mendota), W.C. Bowers (Arlington), Raethie Teer (Dixon), Alma Mae Means (Dixon), and Ruby Thompson (Ladd). Other injured workers were Jewell Druler (Sterling), Mertee Parker (Morrison), Helen Manspeaker (Morrison), and Francis Hall (Vandalia).

When the explosion occurred, the safety officer immediately sounded the alarm, and the line was evacuated within minutes. Flames quickly spread to boxes of loaded rockets.

One of the first responders was Ken Shulte, who removed Mrs. Christy from the area and immediately returned with a fire extinguisher. Shulte, 22, a former Private First Class in the Signal Corps had been given a medical discharge for combat injuries. Upon returning to Dixon, his hometown, he immediately sought a job at GROP. Another individual who was praised for his quick action was a trucker, Charles Sudano of Granville, who helped the wounded get to Judy Hofmann, a nurse at the line's first aid station. Dr. McShane of Spring Valley and his entire medical staff, the guards, fire department, and telephone operators handled the emergency with professionalism and efficiency.

Disaster procedures were immediately put into effect. Fire department personnel rendered first aid. Guards blockaded certain roads, and ambulances were directed to the hospital. Ten nurses were called in from the Dixon public hospital and the Dixon state hospital, while several off-duty GROP nurses hurried back to the plant from their homes in Sterling and Dixon.

One of the loading lines at the Green River Ordnance Plant. Paulsen collection.

Fortunately, damage was very limited. Major Norman Gillespie, the commanding officer at GROP, said that he estimated the property damage "at less than $100, and production was not affected." Line 4, where the accident occurred, was located in a building with 12-inch reinforced concrete walls.

Sabotage was ruled out. Duane Paulsen of Grand Detour, who researched the incident suggested, "The most likely cause was a safety pin missing from a rifle grenade. A group leader said that he found the missing pin on a table when he went into the area after the explosion." Paulsen also suggested a second possible cause of the explosion. "Another story is that the projectile would not go into the (shipping) cylinder, and she tapped it on the end, and it exploded." Paulsen, 14.

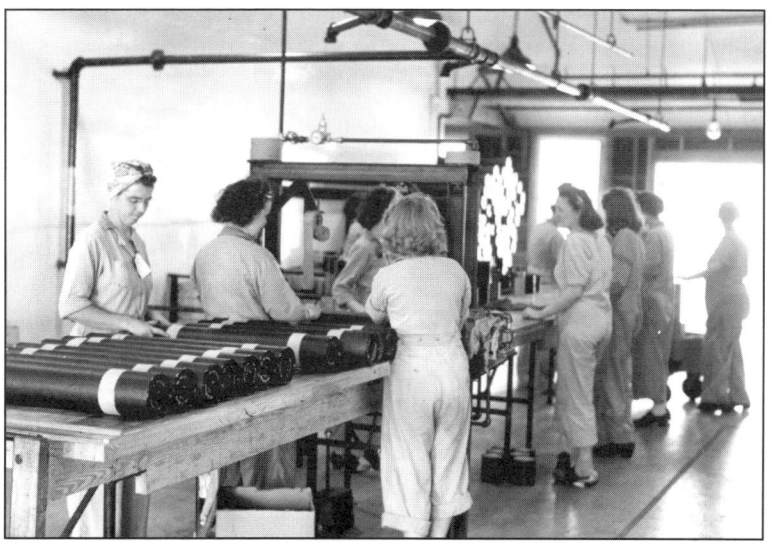

Safety was always emphasized at GROP. (Paulsen collection).

The dedication of the workers to their work could be seen in the rapid return to production. By afternoon, four of the wounded workers were back at their posts packaging more rifle grenades. The Feb. 29 incident was the only fatal injury at GROP.

There were other serious injuries, such as when one worker failed to properly insert a safety pin on a bazooka rocket and caused an explosion. Fortunately, the woman survived. There were also respiratory and skin infection problems caused by explosive dust.

All war plants had to be mindful of safety, but accidents, sometimes fatal, still occurred. Joseph Gore, 50, of LaSalle was killed on Jan. 15 at the Seneca shipyard. The water tender lost his balance and fell 30 feet from the upper deck of an LST. Two more

Seneca workers were killed in April. William Jones, 30, of Oglesby was electrocuted while working on a switchbox on one of the LST's. Dallas Fluegal of Marseilles was killed when the rope slipped on a ventilator being hoisted aboard an LST, and he was crushed. One incident covered by the *Putnam County Record* involved Wallace Dean, a 27 year old Seneca shipyard worker. While on the night shift on June 12, he attempted to move a blower used to ventilate a construction area on an LST. The Magnolia worker apparently came into contact with some high voltage electrical wires and was electrocuted. Wallace was the son of Art and Bertha Wallace of Magnolia and had been working at the Seneca yard for about a year.

Besides safety issues at Seneca, there were also questions being raised about inefficient operations and wasted taxpayer money. Were workers really just standing around with nothing to do? Was the shipyard a refuge for draft-dodgers? Answers were sought to these and other troubling questions by the Putnam County Taxpayers Federation. The group decided to request a first hand inspection of the shipyards. A committee consisting of Joel Hopkins (Granville), Harry Hutton (Magnolia), Charles Robinson (Granville), Joel Whitaker (Granville), Edward Hawthorne (Granville), and J. Lyle Barton, a field representative for the Illinois Taxpayers Federation, traveled to Seneca for a day-long tour of the 192-acre facility.

C.S. Pillsbury, Vice President of Chicago Bridge and Iron, pointed out to the committee that of over 9,500 workers only 630 were between the ages of 18 and 38 making them eligible for the draft. Furthermore, many of them were to be inducted soon. Over 1,000 workers had already left the yards for military service. After working on LST construction, it was understandable why 380 men joined the navy; 12 volunteered for the coast guard; and 45 joined the marines. Another 140 enlisted in the army

The rumor that material was being wasted was also groundless. Wood and metal salvage departments constructed sheds and tool boxes from supplies sent in wooden crates to the yard. Insulation was burned from scrap copper wire so it could be sold. Every month, the Seneca yard brought in an extra $5,000 from the sale of scrap metal. At the end of the day, Hopkins said,

"Our investigation was complete. After we talked with the company and navy officials, we were convinced that the overall job is being well done, although some of us think there could be a more efficient use of manpower."

Meanwhile, the navy had singled out Electrical Utilities in LaSalle for special accolades. The employees had turned out thousands of secret units within four days to fill a special emergency order for the navy. In recognition of that achievement, C.A. Lathier, inspector for the Chicago naval district, praised the workers at an informal dinner at the Hotel Kaskaskia on Mar. 1. Mayor Orr presented a 12-foot American flag to Joseph Marini and Joseph Dolling, who were in charge of raising and lowering the colors every day at the plant. EU President Al Hauser said that the new flag would replace the one currently being used. The older flag presented at the plant dedication in July 1943 would be brought inside and put on permanent display.

On Mar. 22, the Princeton H.S. auditorium was packed to capacity, to hear Mrs. Mark Clark speak. The wife of Gen. Mark Clark, commander of the 5th Army in Italy, was touring the country promoting the Red Cross and war bonds.

Washington constantly asked citizens to purchase more bonds; the USO sought additional funds; and in March, the Tri-Cities' chapter of the Red Cross made a special appeal to raise $26,000. Myron Wallace, the campaign director, admitted that it was the largest amount ever sought locally but said that the need in 1944 was greater than ever. The Tri-City chapter of the Red Cross included not only LaSalle, Peru, and Oglesby but also Tonica, Lostant, Utica, Cedar Point, Waltham, and Dimmick. Each community had a Red Cross center open at least one day a week. In addition, the local Red Cross volunteers had sewn 3,543 garments for use in hospitals; knitted 789 articles for military personnel; and made almost 300,000 surgical dressings.

Red Cross funds were used to maintain canteens, run blood drives, and pay for the shipment of packages to prisoners. That latter service made a lasting impression on the nuns in Spring Valley. One of the most joyful reunions during 1944 involved the return of seven Catholic nuns from St. Margaret's Hospital, who had been held by the Germans in an internment camp in France.

They had gone to the mother house in Broons, France to teach in the early days of the war. When they attempted to return to America by traveling through Spain, they had been stopped at the border. They became prisoners of the Germans and sent to an internment camp. There, the sisters kept busy caring for the hundreds  of sick and elderly. Each nun (pictured above) received a Red Cross package every week from the sisters at St. Margaret's Hospital. Packages contained such items as cheese, margarine, sugar, cocoa, soup, sardines, cigarettes, and tobacco. While the sisters didn't need the last two items, they were able to use them to barter with the Germans to obtain items that made life more tolerable.

Their three-year ordeal ended in March 1944, when the Germans allowed the nuns to board the *SS Gripsholm*, a Swedish exchange ship. Arriving in New York, they were met by Sister Anthony of the hospital staff, who accompanied them back to Spring Valley, where they were welcomed with a tearful reunion on Mar. 20. They expressed sincere thanks for the packages. One nun said, "If it had not been for the Red Cross prisoner of war packages, we could not have appeared as well as we do."

Throughout the war, letters from the front brought hope to those on the home front. Mr. and Mrs. Louis Sartorie of Spring Valley received a letter in March from their son, Cpl. Louis Sartorie, a radioman, describing the details of the successful landings on Kwajalein. Commenting on all the bomb craters in the landing zone, he wrote, "The navy and air force sure did a wonderful job of giving the island a good going over. By the first day we had half the island in our hands and most of the airport."

Many reports from the War Department created anxiety. Howard Salisbury of Tonica received a letter from the War Department on April 9 concerning his son T/Sgt. Frank Salisbury, who was a top turret gunner on the "Virgin Annie," a B-24

Liberator. Salisbury's unit had been on bombing missions over Klagenfurt airdrome and the war plants outside of Graz some 60 miles from Vienna in March, and his plane was reported missing.

More than a month later, the Salisbury's received a phone call from Chicago that stunned the family. When Mrs. Salisbury asked, "Who is this?" the reply was, "This is Frank." Without going into great detail for security reasons, her son explained that he was in Chicago staying with his brother, Maxwell, in Oak Park, IL, and he was coming home to Tonica for the weekend. He said he had gotten back from the mission with only a scratch above his eye. Anxiety gave way to joy and a wonderful reunion with a son. His parents had not seen Frank in seven months.

Not all of the news from the battlefields was as positive. Mr. and Mrs. Clark Briner of McNabb were told that their son, Pvt. Burdette Briner, a paratrooper, was missing in action in Italy. The *Post-Tribune* reported that he was the first McNabb casualty. On Mar. 9, 1944, other news of wounded and missing servicemen was reported in the *Putnam County Record.* Pvt. Angelo Serafini, whose family had moved to Detroit from Mark, was reported wounded in action in the Mediterranean. Mark experienced its first and only fatality on Feb. 21.

Alfonso Piacentini was not informed until Mar. 6 that his son, Second Lt. Irvin Piacentini, (at left) was missing in action in a bombing raid over Germany. The 24-year old pilot was flying a B-17 when his plane came under attack by German fighters. Badly wounded, Piacentini tried to belly land the bomber but was killed on landing near Hiltrup/Westfalen, Germany.

A War Department telegram was also delivered to Mr. and Mrs. Phillip Gordon in Granville informing them that there son, Sgt. Louis Gordon, had been seriously wounded on Feb. 8. Sgt. Gordon (at right) hadn't been allowed a furlough since his induction in Feb. 1942, but instead had been transferred from to Africa, to Sicily and finally Italy. Another telegram reached the Gordon family on Mar. 10 that Louis had died from his wounds on Feb. 29. The 27-year old army sergeant was Granville's first casualty.

The first of the Seneca-built boats, LST 197, took part in the landings in Italy. It was photographed on April 15, 1944 at the little Italian island of Niaida near Naples. Ensign Merlyn F. Burris of Peru, a former athletic coach at L-P-O Junior College, was the navigation officer on the ship. He had been assigned to the ship's crew since the summer of 1943. US Navy photo.

Hennepin families were not immune to bad news. During April 1944, the War Department informed Mrs. Marie Morine that her husband, Merle, an engineer-gunner on a B-24, was missing in action. He had flown over 21 combat missions over Nazi targets. Ironically, the same day the telegram arrived, a letter from Merle was delivered to the Morine home. It was dated Mar. 24, the same day he was reported missing. Enclosed was a photograph of the flyer. On the picture was written "Remember Me."

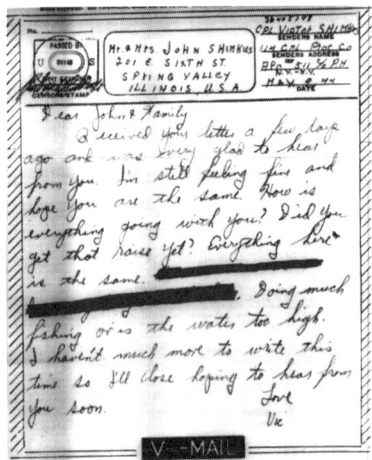

V-mail from servicemen overseas was always reviewed by a censor. His stamp appeared in the upper left hand corner of this May 9, 1944 letter. If some information in the letter was deemed useful to the enemy, the censor blacked it out as seen in this letter. No geographical place names, ships, or unit designations could be mentioned. Letters were also reduced in size to cut the weight of the mail returning to the US. John Shimkus collection.

Most rural families in the Illinois Valley focused on the spring planting of the corn crops. Since LaSalle County produced such abundant corn harvests, the area was designated as one of the 35 surplus corn-producing counties. The Agricultural Adjustment Administration had requested that the county be canvassed for potential farmers who might sell their crops to the government. So, on May 17, Ottawa H.S. was picked for a Corn-for-War show. The purpose of the program was to entice farmers into selling their corn directly to the war industries. Decorated veterans made the pitch to the farmers on behalf of the government.

Not only was the corn itself in demand, but the corn cobs also played a role in winning the war. The Peru Cob Products Co. located on Water Street next to the Burlington freight house had contracted with the federal government to buy large quantities of milled cobs. Scientists discovered that the cobs could be used in making synthetic rubber and other useful products. Farmers would bring the cobs into the Peru plant where they would be ground until they resembled "small popped corn," according to the *Post-Tribune*. The ground cobs were loaded into Burlington box cars and shipped to Memphis, TN and Des Moines, IA, where they were treated with acid to make rubber and other products.

Seneca shipyard won another "E" citation on May 22 and a star for their pennant. Chicago Bridge and Iron photographer Frank Bazzoni wrote in his journal, "This is one of the proudest days for all however connected with the shipyard."

On May 22, LST 619 slid into the Illinois River. The ship was later involved in three major engagements in the Pacific: Leyte, Oct.-Nov. 1944; Lingayen Gulf, January 1945; and Mindanao, April 1945. *Our Prairie Shipyard.*

On the other side of the world, LST's 202 and 204, launched in Seneca in March and April 1943, were unloaded at Leyte. Both ships received numerous battle stars. Coast Guard photo.

At the end of May, there was another recruitment drive in the Tri-Cities. For several weeks, a Spars caravan, consisting of eight enlisted personnel and one ensign, would occupy an office at 620 First Street in LaSalle. A major rally was scheduled for Matthiessen Auditorium at L-P High School for June 6, a date which would be forever remembered in American history, but it was not for the effort to recruit women into the coast guard.

As the historic day approached, the LaSalle Rotary invited the coast guard personnel to a luncheon at the Kaskaskia. Three of the Spars and three men in the military contingent were musically talented and formed the "Coast Guard Cutters," who used their talents to hold the attention of potential recruits. They performed before over 2,000 guests at the LaSalle, Peru, and Majestic theaters. They used the catchy slogan "Don't be a Spare, be a Spar" and told brief stories of their military experiences.

The group also took time to visit the Seneca shipyard to witness the launching of another LST. Tours were also scheduled to Spring Valley and Mendota as part of their recruitment drive.

When the big rally took place at L-P, the atmosphere of the performance had shifted. Instead of a light-hearted, relaxed occasion, the evening began with solemn reflection on the day's events. It was June 6th, D-Day; the invasion of France had begun. For weeks, there had been information leaked to the press about the big military buildup in England for the invasion of France. Another suspicious indicator was that there had been no mail from the British Isles for the last three weeks to insure total secrecy. But on the evening of the Spar rally, the secret was out.

Coast Guard Ensign Theodora Jennings came out on the stage and asked the audience for solemn prayer and reflection. Walter Wagner, secretary of the Chamber of Commerce, also briefly spoke about the events of the day and encouraged the crowd to support the efforts of the Spars. Then everyone stood and sang the "Star Spangled Banner." A film entitled "Task Force," showing how troops established a beachhead, only reinforced the thoughts of anxious parents, who had sons involved in the Normandy landings. Those images, coupled with the descriptions painted by BM3c Melvin Baldwin, who was only one of two men who survived the sinking of the Coast Guard cutter *Escanaba*, added to the seriousness tone of the evening.

The only part of the program that lightened the mood, especially for the younger females in the audience, was the fashion show by the Spars, who wore a variety of uniforms suitable for different occasions. Music by the "Coast Guard Cutters" also relaxed the crowd somewhat as they played both classical and popular tunes.

The Coast Guard group prepared to travel to their next engagement at the Elks in Mendota that evening. They were also thinking of the following night's performance at Hall H.S. But many civilians in the audience had more troubling thoughts.

As early as 2:32 a.m. on June 6th, the LaSalle paper had begun receiving AP news flashes. The *Post-Tribune* teletype machines spewed out the latest information. As quickly as news was received, bulletins were placed in the office window for the few passersby at the early hour. Phone operators at the paper immediately went into action contacting reporters and production personnel. The LaSalle paper ran an extra edition that morning with the headline "Invasion – Allies in France." A few hours later, the regular edition brought Tri-City readers up to date with a new headline, "Allies Driving Into France." Rushing to the plant, one of the editors driving by Westclox stopped just long enough to share the news with a passing worker whose only response was, "No fooling?"

LST's line the Normandy beaches on June 6, 1944. Seneca's LST 197 and 511 were two of the ships approaching the beach on D-Day. US Navy photo.

Seneca-built LST 511 was photographed off the coast of Normandy on D-Day. US Navy photo.

News of the invasion was followed through the day. Eicor employees in Oglesby were brought up to date by their superintendent, Geno Arboit. Radio broadcasts held the attention of guests in hotel lobbies and restaurants. Msgr. L. Bobkiewicz offered a special prayer for the success of the invasion at the morning mass at St. Hyacinth's Catholic Church. Other prayer services were held at 9 a.m. at the Oglesby Baptist Church.

Although there were thousands of soldiers and sailors involved in the landings in Normandy, a few Illinois Valley families were more than just a little concerned for the safety of the servicemen. Lt (j.g.) Donald Bauman, son of Pearl Bauman of Utica, was reportedly aboard the *USS Tuscaloosa,* a flagship for one of the invading groups.

FC Joseph Vene, son of Mr. and Mrs. Anton Vene of LaSalle was thought to be on a cruiser *USS Augusta* (left) US navy photo.

Later, the paper learned that F2c Charles Safranski, son of Mr. and Mrs. Michael Safranski of Oglesby, was aboard the *USS Nevada* (bottom).

Another sailor from Peru, FC3c Orville Walgenbach, was reported to be aboard the *USS Tuscaloosa* (right). US Navy photo.

USS Nevada fired its 14-inch guns in support of the landings on Utah Beach on Dec. 6, 1944. US Navy photo.

The LaSalle paper speculated that many more local men were part of the invasion but had only limited information. One of the first eyewitness accounts of the invasion was reported by F2c Charles Safranski of Oglesby who was aboard the *USS Nevada*. His correspondence with his brother, Ray Safranski of Piety Hill, gave home front readers of the *Post-Tribune* a description seldom revealed in typical V-mail. In his letter, he described the tense moments before dawn on June 6, when the sky was suddenly illuminated by star shells dropped from Allied planes. "Then came the drone of hundreds of bombers and eight miles of exploding bombs on the peninsula that made our ship vibrate. Our air force was at work in spite of the ack ack tracers that made beautiful patterns against the sky." He continued, "The hours melted into days and nights. By daybreak, the allied transports extended from horizon to horizon. While Allied bombers and fighters worked overhead, our guns responded to location data on enemy positions." He closed saying, "Until you hear from me again keep praying, your prayers are being heard."

Coast Guardsman Ed Nosalik of LaSalle got an even better view of the landings since he was on one of the first landing craft to hit the beach. He said, "(Their boat) was nearly swamped from choppy seas breaking over the blunt bow. The soldiers were speechless. They hated that 10-mile ride to the beach. Ahead of us lay the deadly maze of underwater obstacles through which we had to maneuver before unloading the troops. As we crashed through the minefields, we first thought the beach would be a pushover. Not a shot was fired. The defenders had a deadly effective trick of holding fire until we lowered one ramp and the Yanks started to charge." Nosalik said it was "a miracle that we're still alive." Such descriptive reports made those on the home front much more aware of the hazards facing the servicemen.

A month later, the *Post-Tribune* ran stories of the first local casualties of the D-Day invasion. One article told of how Pvt. John Gerdovich of Oglesby was killed during the advance into France on June 10. The former Westclox employee was survived by his parents, Mr. and Mrs. John Gerdovich, his wife, Frances, and their daughter, Patsy. He had two brothers, William and Joseph, in the armed forces and a younger brother, Richard,

14, and a sister, Christine. Another casualty of the invasion was T5 Clement Gillio from Oglesby. His cousin, Pfc. Batista Gillio, was killed on June 5 in Italy. First Lt. Glen Breckenridge was wounded in the hand by a piece of shrapnel during the invasion according to his parents, Mr. and Mrs. Floyd Breckenridge of Lostant. He was one of the first men from the Illinois Valley on the Normandy beaches. He survived the landing but was killed later in the month.

The opening of the second front in France, coupled with the continued fighting in the Pacific, created a serious shortage of workers to harvest crops. William Brenner, who owned the Streator Packing Company, reported at the end of June 1944, that about 30 men from the Caribbean island of Barbados would be employed by his company. Workers were in such short supply, especially during the canning season, that the pumpkin and corn crops were almost lost in past seasons. An arrangement had been worked out between Washington and the governor of Barbados to send 700 workers to the United States. Most of the workers were already in Wisconsin helping with the canning of peas. As soon as that was completed, they would be transferred to other critical areas in Illinois such as Streator. Housing for the workers was arranged in a remodeled building at the corner of Bridge and Illinois Streets. Other Illinois towns with food processing plants needing workers were Sycamore, Hoopeston, Sterling, Princeville, and Rossville.

The war was far from over, and the troop trains continued to travel through Streator, which was a welcomed stop for servicemen and women on Santa Fe trains. For those who had stopped at the canteen on Easter Sunday, there was an added treat, thousands of colored Easter eggs. But it wasn't just the food that made the service club so popular with the troops. Volunteers also phoned parents letting them know that their sons were okay. Donations to the canteen in the form of equipment, materials, and money came from cities, organizations, and the servicemen themselves. In June, the Illinois Valley Horsemen's Association organized by association members in Streator, Ottawa, and Grand Ridge and directed by C. Atlee McCormick, sponsored a Horse Show. It turned out to be one of the most successful shows sponsored by the organization. The profits, amounting to $1,300, were turned over to the canteen. In July, the women from Spring Valley offered to relieve the Streator ladies for a day at Canteen. Five trains were expected, and each train only stopped for about 10-20 minutes. About 2,000 military personnel had to be fed in a single day.

Rather than hold a traditional Fourth of July celebration, it was decided that the Tri-Cities would have a more subdued Independence Day observance. Although employees at banks and small businesses would observe Tuesday as a holiday, many factories stayed open. Gas rationing and a ban on fireworks in LaSalle meant that a lot of residents would probably stay at home to enjoy a peaceful day and quiet evening. Police Chief Peter Walloch said, "This is no time for anyone to be wasting lives, property, and time through needless accidents."

Seneca workers took a brief respite on July 4th to witness the launching of LST 628. The honor of christening the new ship went to Mrs. P.J. Abernathy of Ottawa, who had two sons in the service, Pfc. D.T. Abernathy, who was wounded on Tarawa and received the Silver Star, and Pfc John Abernathy, who was in New Guinea.

At the ceremony, Capt. Wallace Dowd from the Bureau of Ships said to the workers, "Your reputation is worldwide. Everyone knows that the best LST's come from Seneca."

Above and right: LST 628. photos by F.W. Bazzoni.

Few industries were ever awarded the "E" pennants by the War Department, but the Illinois Valley claimed multiple awards for its outstanding productivity. On July 10, William Steinwedell, the general manager of Stewart-Warner, the company operating GROP, received the Army-Navy "E" flag from army Col. Theodore Gerber representing the Under Secretary of War.

Pictured are Col. Gerber, Commander Flint, Lt. Col. Scott, and William Steinwedell. Photo from Paulsen collection.

The ceremony was timed to coincide with the shift change so there was a large crowd from two of the three line shifts. The event was open to the public swelling the crowd on the front lawn in front of the administration building. The GROP color guard then marched to the flagpole and raised the pennant under the Stars and Stripes. Following remarks by Cmdr. J.A. Flint, commander of the naval ordnance plant at Park Ridge, Pvt. Willard Mauksch presented "E" pins to eleven representatives of the employees. Two of those representatives were Frank Waggett and Joseph Caveletto of Spring Valley. The Camp Grant Band then played the national anthem, while the workers sang the "Star Spangled Banner." Little more than a year later, GROP was recognized again and awarded a white star for its "E" pennant.

LST 633 was ready for launching on July 27, 1944. Evelyn Martin had the honor of christening the ship. US Navy photo.

A sense of despondency seemed to affect the men and women working on the LST's at Seneca, or so it was reported. Some could see that the navy contracts would be coming to an end, and they worried about their futures. To shake them out of the doldrums heightened by negative press and radio reports, Donald Leach, the yard manager, sent each worker a motivational letter on July 29, 1944. In his letter titled "Wanted – No Deserters," Leach focused on the need to produce the final 74 ships to mop up the war in the Pacific.

LST 637 was launched on Aug. 18, 1944. US Navy photo.

The Ottawa *Daily Republican* printed part of Leach's letter on July 31, 1944. It read, "We call upon (workers) to stick to their jobs – back up the navy – and prepare to pour on the Japanese the cumulative power of our fleet and our production lines – so that the fleet will be effective and our soldiers and sailors will have the necessary arms and ammunition to take an instant advantage of the opportunities which will be presented to shorten this war." At that time, it was estimated that LST production would continue until the middle of 1945.

Seneca shipyard workers came from many cities in the Illinois Valley. Steve Yusko, John Oleson, Ed Noure, and F.X. Neuman were a few of the workers from Streator. Streatorland Historical Society.

The Steel Control Division at Seneca Shipyards was one small segment of the complex that eventually totaled over 10,000 workers. Streatorland Hist. Society.

Rosalie Fitzkee drenched civilian and military guests on the platform behind LST 645 with a shower of champagne when she christened the new ship on Sept. 20, 1944. Photo by Frank Bazzoni for the US Navy.

One of the important morale boosters during the war for both the military personnel and the families and friends on the home front was the exchange of mail. A former Westclox employee, Pfc. Clarence Washkowiak, USMC, wrote home in the summer of 1944, "I received the Army-Navy E booklet you sent me and was glad to read about the event. About the fuze you are making, I just want to let you know that it is being put to good use. They're sure serving their purposes in many ways. Keep up the good work and keep them coming this way and maybe it wont be so very long until we will be coming your way."

This card was one sent to Pfc. Dale Keilty. For security reasons, only an APO address was known to the sender. John Shimkus collection.

Sept. 28, 1944 marked an auspicious occasion in Seneca. It was the day for the launching of the 100th LST. During a half-hour launching program, former Hollywood actor and current BM2c, Cesar Romero, spoke before a crowd of 8,000 day shift workers. Romero described his service in the Coast Guard aboard an attack transport as it took part in the invasion of Saipan. He said, "After we landed those troops, we had to pull out even without unloading our supplies to avoid a Jap air raid." It was a week later, after heavy naval bombardment, that Romero's ship could unload the supplies. Comparing his experience as a Hollywood actor to the war, he said, "There's nothing make-believe or Hollywood about war." Cesar Romero Photo - *Our Prairie Shipyard*, Oct. 12, 1944.

Thousands of visitors and shipyard workers gathered to listen to Cesar Romero and watch Margaret Johnson christen their 100th LST at Seneca. *Our Prairie Shipyard.*

The Ottawa *Daily Republican* on Sept. 29 reported Romero's remarks about the condition of the wounded marines as they were loaded onto the transport and brought three miles to the island of Tinian. Then, Yard Manager D.A. Leach praised the workers. "LST 647 is the 100th ship to be launched at Seneca. It is a symbol of the progress, achievement, and efficiency of our shipbuilders. This ship represents our part of the blood, sweat, and tears essential to win the war. LST marks 100 down, 57 yet to go. Let us continue this good work and complete the next 57 ships with the same efficiency and determination that marked the efforts for the first 100."

Seneca shipyard workers were given time off to listen to the speeches and watch the christening of LST 647, on Sept. 28, 1944. *Our Prairie Shipyard.*

Left: Mrs. Margaret Johnson christens Seneca's 100th LST. Below: LST 647 slides down the ways into the Illinois River. This ship participated in the fighting at Okinawa in 1945. *Our Prairie Shipyard*

The labor demands at Sampsel Time Controls, the Seneca shipyard, Westclox, Green River Ordnance, and the host of other factories in the Illinois Valley, coupled with the draft, produced a labor shortage.

LST 651 was ready for christening on Oct. 16, 1944. Mary Margaret Aubry was given the christening honors. US Navy photo.

In spite of the demands for both men and women in war plants, volunteers came from near and far to help at Streator's canteen. According to the Streator *Times Press*, groups came from Blackstone, Cornell, Dana, Grand Ridge, Flanagan, Dwight, Gardner, Graymont, Kernan, Kinsman, Leonore, Long Point, Lostant, Morris, Odell, Pontiac, Ransom, Rutland, Saunemin, Seneca, Spring Valley, Tonica, Toluca, Wenona, and others.

Anthony Co. workers also volunteered to work at the canteen. Streatorland Hist. Society.

The fame of the Streator Canteen spread. Radio and movie stars like Amos and Andy, Claudette Colbert, and Shirley Temple (at right), who stopped at the canteen, were amazed at the service provided. Photos-Streatorland Hist. Soc.

Food was served through the windows located at the southeast corner of the Streator depot. Ice cream, cigarettes, and candy bars were added to the standard menu of coffee, cookies, and sandwiches. Streatorland Historical Society.

The Letter Lieutenants from Owens-Illinois Glass in Streator volunteered to work at the canteen one day in November 1944. They served a record-breaking 1,080 soldiers, marines, and sailors. According to their company newspaper, one of the servicemen who stopped that day was a former Owens-Illinois worker from the Glassboro plant. Streatorland Historical Society.

Volunteers from St. Anthony's Church and the Knights of Columbus Auxiliary volunteered groups at the canteen in Nov. 1944.

Refreshments were provided free of charge at the canteen. Streatorland Historical Society.

To offset the financial expenses of the war, the federal government routinely asked for greater sacrifices in the form of additional bond drives. By the summer of 1944, the 5th War Bond Drive was underway.

Within the LaSalle business community, retail clerks were encouraged to promote the bonds. Each clerk received a badge of rank ranging from "private" to "general." Every time a clerk sold a certain amount of bonds, the individual could rise in rank. To be promoted to private first class, a clerk had to sell a $25 bond. The top rank of general required the sale of $5,000 in bonds. Members of the LaSalle Woman's Club, headed by Mrs. Emily Entwistle and Mrs. Charles Hynds, inspected each store to check on sales. Store managers obtained the badges from the Chamber of Commerce.

Every township had a chairman charged with the duty of meeting a set goal. William Harding, the chairman of the drive in LaSalle, explained that the city's quota was $600,000 in actual purchase price not the face amount of the bonds.

As an incentive to reach the goal, local movie theaters were offering a one-month pass for every $100 bond purchased. A special premiere showing of "And the Angels Sing" starring Fred MacMurray and Dorothy Lamour was schedule for a private viewing at 8 p.m. on July 5 at the Majestic and Peru Theaters for those who had purchased a bond. No paid

admissions were allowed for the performance, but several members of the theaters were on hand to sell bonds in the lobby on the night of the performance. According to the LaSalle paper, the scheme was "one of the most successful war bond promotions conducted locally." Over 700 people stood in two lines stretching from the entrance to the Majestic Theater around to the stage door on Second Street for almost an hour waiting for doors to open for the premiere. Bonds worth over $95,000 were sold. Most of the patrons were also eligible for the free pass offered by the management. Last minute patrons bought $7,500 in bonds in the lobby just 90 minutes prior to the screening.

The Princeton Lions Club turned their Rally Day bond sale into a fun-filled event. On Saturday, July 8, Main Street was jammed with thousands of people, according to the *Bureau County Republican*, eager to enjoy the entertainment which included a slave auction as well as musical performers. The afternoon's entertainment began with performances by a number of celebrities including Loretta Linn on the piano and a four-piece combo billed as the "Jumpin' Jeepers." Judge L.A Zearing, the Bureau County bond chairman, was just one of the individuals, who volunteered to go on the auction block to raise money for bonds. Individuals willing to spend $7,000 on bonds were rewarded with a ride in an army jeep. In the evening, radio stars from WLS and WJJD in Chicago along with a variety show of local and national talent was showcased. Barbara Ann Traynor sang "America Needs You Now," a recently published tune for which Lillian Ruttan of Princeton wrote the lyrics, and Hugh Price of Kewanee composed the music. By the end of the day, the Citizen's National Bank had collected almost a quarter of a million dollars for the 5th War Loan.

In Putnam County, Benjamin Holye of McNabb was in charge of raising $277,000. Harry Hutton led the effort in Magnolia Township to meet its $70,000 goal. John P. Dore and Lyle E. Morine had a smaller goal, $35,000 in bond sales in Hennepin Township. Three others, Howard Dysart, Leo Utterback, and Ken Edgerly, faced the greatest task, securing $75,000 in bond pledges in Granville Township. The bond drive in Senachwine Township was headed by Francis Murphy and Guy French. Their quota was set at $30,000. To round out the grand total, an additional $67,000 in corporate bond pledges was expected for the county. The same sort of effort was expected in every county.

By July 31, Peru had met its $400,000 quota and exceeded it by more than $21,000, according to Andrew Hebel, chairman of the Peru drive. He said his committee was pleased with the cooperation from Peru citizens who showed they "were 100 percent behind the boys fighting at the front." Harding, chairman in LaSalle, also expressed his gratitude saying, "It was a wonderful response to our government's call." LaSalle had already purchased $737,000 in bonds, far exceeding their quota of $600,000.

While the bond drive was in progress, OPA decided to issue a new ration book for gas purchases. The old "A" books had to be turned in when drivers registered for the new edition, which the OPA planned to release on Sept. 1. Although the standard allotment of eight gallons a month had not changed, OPA decided to make each coupon worth four gallons instead of three. Every month another set of six four-gallon coupons would become valid. To further confuse motorists, the government agency decided to use a new Mileage Rationing Record to replace the Tire Inspection Record. The new document would be needed when requesting a special or supplemental ration.

Those who relied on cars for transportation in the Tri-Cities were also facing serious tire shortages. On July 25, Henry Vroman, chairman of the local rationing board warned, "Unless every operator keeps his tires in good repair and has them recapped and vulcanized before it is too late, there is going to be a good percentage of cars and trucks that will be forced off the roads in the months to come. Manufacturers' and dealers' stocks of new tires are practically exhausted. Used tires are just about a thing of the past. The truck tire situation is even worse than the passenger tire shortage." Vroman predicted that there might be a 50 percent drop in production of new tires due to shortages of labor and the demands of the military.

Taxi cab drivers actually had to suspend service for a short time at the end of June due to the lack of gas ration stamps. Applications for a supplemental gas ration were denied at the Peoria office. Only through the efforts of Walter Wagner of the Chamber of Commerce did the Office of Defense Transportation reconsider the denial and approve the request.

A potentially devastating railroad incident occurred in Mendota on July 20 at 11:50 p.m. One of the trucks on a car about 20 cars behind the engine of the eastbound Burlington freight cut loose at the Burlington-Illinois Central crossover. This caused the last 11 cars to overturn, spilling their contents across the Sixth Street junction. According to the *Mendota Reporter*, one car was carrying munitions. "If the contents had exploded, the consensus of opinion is that there would not be very much of Mendota left to tell the story." (*Note - The LaSalle Daily Post-Tribune reported that several cars were carrying explosives.*)

There were several eyewitnesses, who described the event. George Wagner, who was in charge of the switches, thought the cars were going to crash into the switch tower. Although they tore up the tracks all the way to the Sixth Street crossing, the derailed cars missed the tower. J.H. Walker, who was walking along the tracks saw a fiery flash, six feet long and heard a terrible rumbling. He said cars were going in all directions, and there was a loud crack when an airbrake hose snapped. The trucks on the derailed cars were torn out at the switch tower. Frank Seno, another eyewitness, also saw the flash followed by a cloud of dust caused by the grinding of the cars being pulled along without their wheels. One of the cars ended up on the northbound Illinois Central tracks.

Railroad crews brought huge cranes from Aurora and Galesburg and worked all day and into the night to remove the wreckage. Residents coming into town found a roped-off area three blocks around Sixth Street. All traffic on the Burlington and Illinois Central lines was stopped. Temporary tracks were laid, and by 7 a.m., the first Burlington trains were cautiously moving across the new tracks. A preliminary investigation of the accident concluded that a load had shifted in one of the cars as the train rounded the curve where the accident occurred.

Recycling was one of the continuous efforts to solve the numerous shortages. Oglesby City Clerk Edward Hand announced a waste paper drive was planned for Aug. 2 to coincide with a county-wide effort. Children were to bring bundles to the fire house, and for every 50 pounds, they would be given one of the 200 free tickets to the National Barn Dance at the Ottawa H.S. gym on Aug. 8. The 2½-hour children's show would be at 4 p.m. followed by two adult shows. The only way to be admitted to the shows was by bringing in 50 pounds of paper.

Mayor Orr of LaSalle also got behind the wastepaper drive saying, "Let's all get behind this county-wide drive so that no one can say LaSalle did not do its part. Wastepaper is today's number one critical war shortage. Without paper to pack ammunition, medical, and food supplies our armies cannot receive them properly so as to continue the advances they are now making." Tickets in LaSalle were available at the Ramenovsky junk yard and in Peru at Tom Lyons Implement shop. All of the money raised went to the LaSalle County War Service fund.

Princeton was also very involved in the various salvage drives. Mrs. Ed Dahl was handling the tin can drive at the end of July. In August, the Bureau County Rural Youth organization, 4-H, and Boy Scouts volunteered to assist in the wastepaper drive being promoted by the War Production Board. The government agency explained that there was a shortage of 300,000 loggers and mill workers; supplies of wood pulp from Sweden and Finland were cut off; and it took a tremendous amount of paper products – 25 tons just for the blueprints for a single battleship – to meet the needs of the military. By the time the Princeton drive was finished, 65 tons of paper was collected.

War production workers were constantly urged to avoid absenteeism if at all possible. The War Manpower Commission singled out Henrietta Schmoeger of LaSalle for special recognition as an outstanding war worker at a special program in Chicago on July 28. She was employed as a condenser assembler at Electrical Utilities in LaSalle. The mother of five sons in the navy represented the thousands of Tri-City workers who had maintained an unusually low rate of absenteeism.

Summertime concerts in the Illinois Valley reflected both patriotism on the home front and support for the armed forces. On Aug. 8, a concert dedicated to the men and women in the armed forces from Peru was held in Washington Park. The color guard consisted of discharged WWII veterans, who were members of American Legion Post 375. Musical selections by the combined American Legion and municipal bands included "The Caissons Go Rolling Along," "Anchors Aweigh," "What Do They Do in the Infantry," and "The WAC is a Soldier Too," as well as the "Star Spangled Banner." Throughout the program, time was taken to honor deceased veterans of WWII and listen to remarks by army and navy personnel.

One of the biggest local events during the summer of '44 was a two-hour concert at the L-P High School football stadium to honor Westclox workers. For weeks, stories described the Aug. 22, admission-free event sponsored by Coca Cola. It was all part of a national radio program series featuring the Coca Cola "Spotlight Band," the nationally known Bob Chester Orchestra.

On the day of the concert, the weather was threatening, and planners could not decide whether to move the performance into the L-P gym or hope that the weather would clear. One thousand of the 3,000 chairs set up on the football field were moved to the gym when rain began to fall at 5:30 p.m. Fortunately, the rain clouds moved off, and the chairs were hastily moved back to the field; tarps covering the piano and broadcasting equipment were quickly removed.

Another vexing problem for promoters was the late arrival of the orchestra, which had missed its scheduled train from Chicago. There was no room for the band on the next *Peoria Rocket*, so a bus and some station wagons were used to transport the musicians to LaSalle.

The appearance of the stadium left no doubt as to the purpose of the event. According to the *Post-Tribune*, the background of the bandstand was draped with a red and green backdrop featuring "the smiling face of the Coca Cola capped boy, while the football scoreboard above was covered with a large panel on which was a picture of Big Ben and the words 'Salute to Westclox'."

More than 5,000 guests jammed the stadium when the show finally began at 8:20 p.m. Before the performance, Westclox officials and Al and Andrew Hebel of the local Coca Cola bottling company were introduced. The musical program was interrupted from time to time to allow Wayne Griffin, the announcer, to describe the important bomb parts and other war equipment made by Westclox. The coast-to-coast broadcast was being piped into the Westclox lunch room, but some of the swing shift employees walked the two blocks to the stadium to watch the program from the south rim. After the 30-minute broadcast portion of the music spectacle concluded, Bob Chester's Orchestra continued with another hour-long program.

Yet another musical extravaganza was offered on Sept. 1, at the L-P stadium. Drum Major Geraldine Hopp from L-P High School was in charge of the entire pageant, including the direction of the state champion high school band, and the coordination of the elementary school bands from Peru, LaSalle, and Oglesby – a total of 200 musicians. She was later presented with a gold medal for selling 80 tickets to the show.

Like previous pageants, the emphasis was once again focused on patriotism. The marching bands formed into the letter "M" and played the marine hymn. Next, they formed an "N" to honor the navy while playing "Anchors Aweigh." The marchers repositioned themselves to form the letters "A-C" for the Army Air Corps and played the Air Corps March. Before breaking formation, they played "Taps" to honor those who had died in the war. The finale came with the marchers forming the letters "USA" surrounded by a map of the United States. The stadium lights were extinguished, leaving only red, white, and blue torches to outline the "USA" formation. During the playing of the "Star Spangled Banner," rockets were fired from the north end of the stadium exploding overhead with dazzling displays of red showers.

While the martial music, patriotic speeches, and various awards presentations gave local communities a sense of unity and direction, it was the day-to-day production in the war plants that had a more direct effect on the progress of the war on the home front. Factories, such as Westclox, were desperately in need of more employees to assemble the fuses for a variety of ordnance.

Full page ads were run in the *Post-Tribune* exhorting any available worker to sign up for employment. It spite of wartime secrecy, it was widely known that the plant made fuses for low level parachute fragmentation bombs, incendiary bombs, demolition bombs, and flares. The management suggested adjusting family commitments so one or two members could work at the Peru plant. An Aug. 31 article in the LaSalle paper concluded, "Recent news from the battle fronts has given people at home complacency. This war is not yet won. On the contrary, the demand for front-line weapons, such as Westclox makes, is greater than ever."

Personal stories of experiences from military personnel stationed overseas gave friends and families some insights about life in distant lands. Illinois Valley newspapers frequently printed letters from servicemen, but specific details of military operations were still classified. Usually, the servicemen just described their new surroundings and unique lifestyles. Typical was an innocuous letter from Bill Kostellic printed in the July 27th *Putnam County Record*. Kostellic described everyday life in Australia explaining the local expressions such as ordering a "pot" of beer instead of a glass of beer. He also said he had to get used to local monetary terms like "bob" and "quid" instead of shillings and pounds.

A letter from M/Sgt. Jeno Bonucchi of Granville described his routine in India, where malaria was a major problem in the rainy season. He said, "I have insect repellent all over me but it seems to attract them instead of driving them away." He also provided some insights about his work in maintaining the C-47's and C-46's (below) flying over the "hump"– the Himalayas – to bring supplies to the Flying Tigers in China. He described how on one occasion, the crews flew 189 missions to China in a single day. Bonucchi said the commander "was very pleased with the results."

While these accounts were interesting, the casualty stories made people in the Illinois Valley realize that the war zone could be very dangerous and not simply an intriguing or exotic place to visit. Smaller communities felt the loss of one of their own in a very personal way. Granville residents took special note of the death of Cpl. Raymond Baxter, a graduate in the Hopkins H.S. Class of '34 and recent employee at American Nickeloid in Peru. He had been killed in France on July 11 and was the second casualty in the town, Sgt. Louis Gordon having been the first death in Feb. 1944. Within a week, Granville residents were also troubled by the news that another local man, Tech Sgt. William Kibble, the son of Mr. and Mrs. William Kibble, was missing in action. Sgt. Kibble, a radio operator on a B-17, was reported lost on a mission over Germany.

Another story in the *Bureau County Republican* on July 13, told how Pfc Dallis Prather of Princeton sacrificed his life in the Battle of San Pietro (Italy) to save the lives of the other 47 men in his unit. He was posthumously awarded the Distinguished Service Cross for gallantry.

Hardly a day passed without a story about another soldier in the Illinois Valley being killed or wounded. Such losses were noted in every community, but workers continued their day-to-day work on the farms and in factories hoping that their work might bring the war to a speedy conclusion.

Factory workers at the Anthony Hydraulic Co. in Streator built a variety of bomb carriers, trailers, and truck beds for the military during WWII. The Anthony Company's *Shop News*, was filled with letters from former employees who were now in the armed forces. They often mentioned how frequently they spotted various types of equipment manufactured by the Anthony Co. They also remarked that the equipment made their jobs much easier.

Pictured are some of the workers in the Assembly Department at the Anthony Co. in Streator.

Moving bombs on Majero Island was made much easier with carriers made by the Anthony Co. US Navy photo, *Shop News,* Sept. 1944.

Photos of the use of bomb carriers were released by the US Navy and Coast Guard for publication in the Anthony Co. magazine. Streator workers at the Anthony Co. built these bomb carriers being used to load Douglas Dauntless SBD dive bombers in the Marshall Islands. US Navy photo in the Anthony Co. *Shop News*, Sept. 1944.

When American forces took the island of Bougainville, the steel sections needed for the landing strip were loaded into truck beds made by the Anthony Co. *Shop News*, June 1944. USMC photo.

It wasn't just the work at the welding stations and assembly lines making trailers, truck beds, and bomb carriers that made the contribution of the Anthony workers notable on the home front. They also took their turn serving at the Free Canteen. Photo – Nov. 1944, Streatorland Historical Society.

While the Anthony Co. and Owens-Illinois were two of the major companies tied to war contracts, there were a number of other companies, which either directly or indirectly contributed to the war effort. The furnaces of the Streator Brick Company were used to temper armor plate on Sherman M-4 tanks. In addition, the link pins for the tank tracks and bushings for all models of tanks were hardened at the Streator facility. The Streator Manufacturing Co. produced wooden wheels for bomb trailers, wooden grease wheels for the army, and tool boxes for the navy. The J. Edgar Noonan Co. in Sterling Hall manufactured cushions for special navy truck bodies. G&D Manufacturing, Schroeder Foundry, Streator Drain Tile, and the Clausen Machine Shop were all designated as essential war industries.

The War Department purchased 60 percent of the asparagus, corn, and pumpkin production at Streator Canning. Sixty percent of the output of canned asparagus from Klinedell Canning Co. on Coalville Road and a similar amount of the canned meats from Streator Meat Packing went to the navy.

Although it was only September, the Marseilles Mothers, Wives, and Friends of Servicemen's Club began packing and shipping 25 boxes to be shipped overseas. It cost about $2 for every parcel, but the Marseilles Painters Union Local 1109 donated $25 to help with the postage. It was just a start since there were 700 men in the service from Marseilles.

On Sept. 8, the OPA announced that there was going to be a change in the seven-month use of the blue and red tokens used in the rationing system. Effective Oct. 1, all blue tokens would be scrapped because most canned foods were no longer rationed. All ration points would be in multiples of ten. Any left over blue tokens could be used in multiples of ten. Red tokens would still be used for meat and dairy products.

There had been widespread theft of gas coupons. Locally, an incident occurred on Rt. 52 at Troy Grove. Richard Palmer's service station was robbed of a nickel slot machine, whiskey, and cigarettes in addition to a bowl of "A" coupons. Perhaps it was the proliferation of illegal gas coupons that led to another directive issued by the OPA. The old "A" coupons were no longer accepted. New "A" coupons would be valued at 4 gallons each. The Ottawa ration board added that stubs from the applications for the new "A" coupons would serve as identification. In the past, residents making such applications had to present their tire inspection records before the gas coupons would be authorized.

During September 1944, the navy made an appeal to young people through area newspapers to pick milkweed pods. Open-mesh collection bags were distributed through schools, 4-H organizations, the Boy Scouts, and other groups. In LaSalle County, School Superintendent Willard Foster sent a letter to every rural school explaining the need for the milkweed floss. The navy was going to use the floss to replace kapok in life jackets. The kapok floss from the silk-cotton tree had been imported from the island of Java, which was occupied by the Japanese. All other supplies had been exhausted. So the navy found that the floss from milkweed pods was the best substitute. Foster hoped that each school in the county would return at least a half sack of the dried pods. Teachers were to bring the bags to a meeting held on Oct. 27. Members of 4-H, who collected pods, would make their reports to George Trull at the Farm Bureau office in Ottawa. The government paid 20 cents for every bag of dried pods.

While the students were collecting the milkweed pods for the navy, the navy decided to do something for two local high schools. During the course of the war, the navy had bought many new airplanes, but not all performed as well as expected. One type was the Curtiss SO3C "Seamew" (at left). Only 794 of these two-man navy scout planes, originally designated as "Seagulls," were built. Most SO3C's were fitted with pontoons (pictured below) and were designed to be catapulted from battleships or cruisers, but the Curtiss Seamews did not live up to expectations. Instead of scrapping the floatplanes, the navy decided to loan some of the single-engine scouts to high schools.

On Sept. 13, 1944, the *Republican-Times* reported that Ottawa H.S. would receive one of the planes. Ben Rotter, the metals class instructor, was responsible for getting the plane, which would be stored in the Manual Arts Building. George Willy was going to use the plane in his pre-flight classes. The school also received three extra engines including a 14-cylinder Pratt and Whitney radial engine, a 9-cylinder Pratt and Whitney engine, a 12-cylinder Ranger engine, and other aircraft equipment such as carburetors, magnetos, ignition mock-ups, propellers, and tachometers. LaSalle-Peru H.S., which had a course in aeronautics for the past three years, also received a SO3C on Sept. 13. The two planes had been used by the naval cadets at Navy Pier for flight training on aircraft carriers. L-P and Ottawa would be the only two high schools in the area to receive the planes.

Another well-intentioned plan by the government, making rope from hemp, also had questionable results. The farmers involved in hemp production soon realized that there wasn't much future in the crop. Even though the hemp was planted again in the spring on about 4,000 acres around Earlville, Polo, Galva, Lexington, and Kirkland, the 1943 crop was still not processed until August 1944 at the Earlville plant. The processing plants at Wyoming and Ladd were also ready to take the 1943 crop out of storage and send the stalks through the grinding machines to separate the strands to make rope. No hemp was raised near the Ladd plant in 1944, and there was little prospect for government contracts for 1945. In October 1944, the Reconstruction Finance Corporation finally decided to sell or lease the land and hemp processing buildings in Wyoming and Ladd. All the elaborate planning and money that went into the hemp growing project turned out to be a government boondoggle.

One government project that was meeting expectations was the Green River Ordnance Plant near Amboy. Production demands were overwhelming the workforce. So, a special effort was made to interest potential additional employees on October 24. The Sixth Army Command, in conjunction with the War Manpower Commission, sponsored an all-day event in Princeton. Commenting on the program, General Chairman Samuel Traynor said, "We're bringing soldiers and some of the very artillery and weapons being used on all fronts so that people can see as well as read about the firepower the Army needs."

When the army arrived on Tuesday, they brought with them some of the armored vehicles typically used in the battles described in the newspapers. Among the 30 vehicles on display was an M-10 tank destroyer, a 30-foot amphibious dukw (duck), and a half track on which was mounted a 37mm gun. Other equipment on display included a 105mm howitzer, a 75mm gun, a 37mm anti-tank gun, and a 40mm Bofors anti-aircraft gun. Refreshments were provided by the Beta Sigma sorority at the Alexander Park dance pavilion. Meals for the 125 soldiers were prepared by the ladies of the English Lutheran Church. *Bureau County Republican* ad.

In the evening, the crowd packed the auditorium of Princeton H.S. Over 1,000 people had to be turned away. Those who managed to find a seat enjoyed demonstrations of the use of attack dogs and judo techniques as well as performances by a variety of musicians, dancers, and singers. Music was provided by the 347th Army Service Forces Band from Fort Custer, MI. The day's events closed with a two-hour dance at the park pavilion.

The efforts of the day seemed to have paid off in their intended consequences. Over 100 people signed the "interested list" so they could be contacted for job interviews at the Green River plant. Capt. Acheson, the caravan's commander, told the *Bureau County Republican,* during their 15 engagements, Princeton had provided the best treatment to date.

The following month on Nov. 28, the Army Air Corps was in LaSalle at the L-P auditorium. The LaSalle Retail Merchants Bureau, under the direction of Chairman Paul Knight, sponsored a performance by the Army Air Force's WACaravan. The two-hour show was packed with music, dance, and comedy skits featuring many talented performers, who had performed with big name bands such as the Sammy Kaye Orchestra. Cpl. Jerry Ziering was billed as the "Harry James of the AAF." Another performer was Cpl. Tony Costello, a former singing partner with Frank Sinatra.

In Putnam County, Judge Albert Pucci of Hennepin was busy trying to organize the Illinois War Fund to finance USO activities. The drive began on Oct. 9. Ed Daubs from Magnolia Township, J.B. Crandall from Senachwine Township, and Raymond Munks of Hennepin Township had agreed to serve with Judge Pucci. The quota set for the county was raised to $3,219.

The final days of collections for the National War Fund were coming to an end on Dec. 1, but LaSalle had already beaten its quota of $13,000. Marseilles was only $120 shy of its goal. Ottawa was also trailing in contributions. The board of directors of the drive released a statement reported in the *Post-Tribune* on Nov. 24, 1944, saying. "As always LaSalle leads. Our thanks are only surpassed by the servicemen who will reap the benefits through USO entertainment, by our men in Axis prison camps, and by those in foreign countries who will receive a share.

The *Daily-Post* used the occasion of Dec. 7, 1944 to review the human cost of the war in the Illinois Valley. According to the paper's best figures, in the Tri-Cities alone 64 men had been killed; 14 were MIA's; and another 14 were POW's. The paper did not list the casualties from Ottawa but did cite the following numbers of men who had lost their lives: Spring Valley - 8, Princeton - 6, Mendota - 5, DePue - 5, Cherry - 3, Lostant - 3.

While the death toll was smaller in surrounding towns, hardly a single community was spared the loss of one or two soldiers. McNabb was the only town of record that had not lost a man. However, the town did have two men being held as prisoners. Casualty reports changed those numbers constantly.

Farmers north of Peru were unaccustomed to military aircraft flying over Rt. 51. However, on the evening of Dec. 13, around 6 p.m., a navy pilot on a routine training mission became lost. He decided to try to land his plane in a farm field rather than parachute and lose his plane. His plan almost worked, but the plane's wheels hit a furrow causing the aircraft to flip over. The uninjured pilot made his way to the John McCabe farmhouse four miles north of Peru. McCabe took the pilot to Peru, where he phoned the authorities at his base, the Glenview Naval Air Station. The next day, navy personnel came to the crash site and dismantled the plane to take it back to the base.

Capt. Anthony Faletti M.D. of Oak Park was one of the servicemen returning for a medical furlough at Christmas. He had only a few days to visit his brother, Stephen, in LaSalle, and other friends in Spring Valley. In an interview with the *Post-Tribune*, he told about his life on Hollandia, where he was assigned to a combat hospital. Dr. Faletti said he had to sleep in a rain-filled foxhole covered by mosquito netting. While working in the jungle, where it rained for as long as four hours at a time, he contracted arthritis in his elbows, hands, and knees. He also said that the natives were very shrewd traders and would exchange war souvenirs and Japanese prisoners for K-rations. The islanders convinced the Japanese soldiers that they were being taken to a Japanese hospital when, in reality, they were being taken to the American lines. Once in captivity, the enemy soldiers naively provided information about their units since they were never taught to only reveal their names and serial numbers.

As the year came to an end, Illinois Valley businessmen described their companies' roles in the war at various luncheons. Dale Peterson, superintendent of the Philadelphia Quartz Co. located east of Utica described the importance of his company's production of waterglass, better known to chemists as sodium silicate. The product, originally used in the manufacture of soap, found a use in the war effort as a coating for the welding rods used at places like Seneca shipyard. It was also a necessary ingredient in the production of high octane gasoline, water purification, and the fabrication of cardboard boxes and grinding wheels.

Mining and processing minerals didn't have quite the glamour and ceremony as launching a ship at Seneca or carefully loading bombs at Amboy, but it was still a vital wartime endeavor. Speaking at a year-end Rotary Club meeting at the Kaskaskia hotel, Charles MacBrayne, superintendent of the M&H Zinc Co. in Peru, described how the company processed 32,000 tons of zinc from ore shipped in from Missouri, Wisconsin, Idaho, and Washington. One of the byproducts of producing zinc was sulfuric acid, a vital product in wartime.

CHAPTER FIVE
Final Push to Victory

View of the Seneca shipyard, Feb. 23, 1945.

On Jan. 2, 1945, the new year at Seneca began with the christening of LST 1117 by Mrs. Angeline C. Pattelli of 103 Eleventh Street in Peru. Mrs. Pattelli's family was very involved with the war. Her husband, Primo, who was a hull fitter at the Seneca yard, had four brothers in the service. Sgt. Emil Pattelli saw combat in Guadalcanal and Bougainville. Another brother, Steve, was an army sergeant being held as a POW by Germans. Quinto Pattelli was in the navy as was a fourth brother, Carlo, who had been assigned to LST duty for three months and then transferred to a destroyer, which was involved in the invasions at Tarawa, Guam, and Saipan. Mrs. Pattelli had four brothers in the service. Two brothers, John and Joseph Colmone, were assigned to the First Army fighting in Europe. James was serving in the Dutch East Indies, and Samuel was assigned to a base in New Mexico with the Army Air Corps. *(Note- On June 5, 1945, LST 1117 was converted to a Landing Craft Repair Ship ARL-27 and rechristened USS Tantalus.)*

The cover of the Chicago Bridge and Iron magazine, *Our Prairie Shipyard*, on Feb. 28, 1945, illustrated the unceasing home front effort to complete the production of another LST on schedule in spite of the cold weather at the Seneca shipyard.

It required two cranes to place the upper bow section of an LST in position. *Our Prairie Shipyard.*

Whether it was LST's from Seneca, ammunition trailers from Streator, flare fuses from Peru, torpedo detonators from Spring Valley, or the artillery shells from Amboy, the sailors and soldiers depended on the unending supplies coming from the Illinois Valley home front.

Soldiers in Brest, France load artillery shells into one of the Anthony Company's M-10 carriers. Anthony's *Shop News*, Jan. 1945 Photo – U.S. Signal Corps.

These welders at the Anthony Co. fought the Axis from Streator, while others used the equipment they produced to fight the war in the Pacific and Europe. Anthony Co. *Shop News*, 1945.

Bomb carriers and trailers from the Anthony Co. were used to move ordnance to B-25's on Kwjalein, US Navy photos, Anthony Co. *Shop News,* April 1945.

The cost of the war, whether it was for tanks, ships, planes, bombs, or the salaries for the military, required more and more money. The new 6th War Loan was going strong in late 1944 as local funds poured in. Everyone seemed to go all out to beat whatever quotas were set. LaSalle, for instance, was supposed to raise $625,000 but had pledges of $765,384 by January 1945. Peru also went "over the top." Originally, Andrew A. Hebel, who was in charge, faced a daunting goal of $400,000. The total came in at $525,309 – 30 percent more than the quota! Oglesby did the same thing. The city's quota was $100,000, but the final pledge count totaled $138,335.

In spite of the determined efforts of the factory workers, farmers, and civic volunteers, the sacrifices on the home front could not compare to those on the battlefields. In Putnam County, Magnolia residents read about their second war casualty. Pfc. E. Farling was reported missing in action just before Christmas. The community's first loss was Pvt. Robert Ahlstrom, who was killed in the South Pacific in 1944.

First hand accounts of the fighting were delayed for weeks. Back in the winter of '44, the papers were filled with reports of the Battle of the Bulge, but it wasn't until late January when a personal account of the fighting was described in letters from Pvt. Eric Erickson to his wife, Estelle, and parents, Mr. and Mrs. Uno Erickson of Deer Park. Pvt. Erickson's unit had been pushed back to Bastogne, Belgium on Dec. 17. His outfit was trapped at Moarch, Luxemburg, where they endured a murderous 72-hour German bombardment. Wounded by a piece of shrapnel, he and 15 other men from his division managed to escape at the end of December. Having lost their overcoats and dressed only in light jackets, they trudged through water over their boots. He said, "My Christmas dinner was pieces of rye bread and an apple. It was a Christmas I shall never forget." Erickson finally made it to a rest camp in France.

Home front citizens didn't have to face that kind of sacrifice even though some products were harder to buy. OPA froze all sales of lard, and cooking oils. Butter and margarine were already being rationed, but the new items were frozen due to a fear that there would be a run on the items before they could be assigned a point value. Once word of a freeze was announced, hotels and restaurants in the Illinois Valley agreed to cooperate by reducing the amount of butter they served with typical meals to 50 percent of what was normal. In LaSalle-Peru, all butter was to be eliminated from sandwiches, and none would be available for doughnuts or sweet rolls. Instead, customers would be offered cottage cheese or jelly. For the consumer, there would be no change from the three red points required for the purchase of margarine – at least through February. This was to discourage the use of butter in cooking. Butter was at the top of the list of rationed products requiring 24 points for one pound. The points for pork products were also going up. The *Post-Tribune* reported, "Plate and jowl bacon, pork fat backs, and clear plates, jowls, jowl butts or squares . . . will require a point."

The War Production Board also issued new regulations. Effective February 1, every community was required to participate in a "brown-out." The plan to turn off all illuminated window and outdoor advertising signs was put into effect in order to conserve coal. The WPB expected all neon signs and theater marquee lights to be turned off. Even illuminated outdoor clocks, church bulletin boards, and illuminated military service honor rolls came under the directive. Street lights, traffic signals, and lighting for hospitals and doctors offices, and railroad and bus depots would not be extinguished, but they would be limited to bulbs of no more than 60 watts. In cooperation with the directive, Illinois Power Co. requested the LaSalle police to report any violations.

After the first night of the brown-out, it was determined that there were quite a few businesses violating the rule. Although the majority of Oglesby and Peru business complied, LaSalle service stations in particular were flaunting the directive. When questioned as to why they were not cooperating, station owners said that competing stations had not done it. Oglesby Police Chief John Spelich reported 100 percent compliance. All display signs, as well as the marquee at the Aida Theater, were turned off. The lights for the marquee at the State Theater in Mendota were out, but one 60-watt light bulb was allowed to illuminate the entrance.

In the nights that followed, there were still a few gas stations in violation of the regulation. Three had their brand name signs illuminated, and one of those also kept on the neon lights advertising lube service and repairs. The only lights allowed at gas stations were those to illuminate the driveway and overhead canopies. The illuminated globes on top of the pumps had to be turned off as well. Illinois Power threatened to turn off the electricity to stations that continued to break the rule.

In spite of these inconveniences, most people were willing to make sacrifices especially for those in the service. For instance, workers at Eicor had formed the Servicemen's Club as early as 1943 to raise funds to buy gifts for the former employees in the military. Included in the packages were copies of "Ripples," the company magazine, and small gifts like "The Kit Book," a collection of novelettes, stories, and cartoons.

In 1945, the Eicor club was headed by Ed Walters. Other officers were Lee Parisotto and Mary Vasicak. A committee consisting of Rita Moalli, Rena Parisotto, Jerry Arkels, and Alex McPhedran was organized to purchase different items. Alice Kutz, another club officer, reported in January that the club had received short letters of appreciation for the small duffel bags containing shaving cream, tooth paste, foot powder, and similar items. Other men received stationery, soap, and sewing kits. Boxes of candy, fruit cake, and nuts were also sent at Christmas. Each serviceman, who had worked at Eicor, also received a wallet engraved with the man's name and the club name.

The generosity of Illinois Valley residents extended beyond gifts to servicemen. On Feb. 27, the nationwide organization of school superintendents was sponsoring its fourth annual Children's Clothing Crusade, which was designed to assist the Save the Children Federation. Although half of the clothing collected was earmarked for impoverished children in America, the other half went to war-torn Europe. In 1944, 50,000 pounds of children's clothing went to refugees in Norway and Finland and other substantial amounts went to Yugoslavia. A goal of 2.5 million pounds was established for 1945. At L-P High School, Superintendent Frank Jensen hoped that every student would contribute to the campaign.

Another collection drive was aimed at bringing in more tin cans. T.P Parlon, the WPB salvage representative for LaSalle County, explained that the tin was needed, as in the past, to make individual morphine hypodermic syringes, which were almost 100 percent pure tin. Containers made of tin were also used by medics to protect plasma and to encase sulfa ointments. Parlon emphasized his plea for volunteers stating, "Tin saves lives" The tin can drive was scheduled for March 17.

The greatest sacrifices were felt by those who received news of the death of a serviceman. In Granville, word was finally received that Pvt. James Boyd had been killed in Germany on Nov. 30, 1944. His survivors included his wife, Hazel (Greathouse), who worked at the shipyard, and two young sons,

Richard, and Ronald. Other family members resided in Oglesby, Spring Valley, and Tonica. Another casualty in Putnam County was Cpl. Ellsworth Reavy, a native of Hennepin. He had been reported missing on Sept. 19, 1944, but the War Department did not confirm his death until the middle of February 1945. Two of his brothers, Clifton and Robert, had been wounded. Another brother, James, was still fighting somewhere in Europe.

The community of Ladd shared the pain of war when news arrived that Cpl. Lester Pinter (at right) was killed. On Feb. 24, 1945, the Marine Corps medic had distinguished himself by crawling through a mortar barrage to bring aid to the wounded and staying with them through a night of Japanese bombardment on their position on Corregidor. On Feb. 24, he was awarded the Silver Star. Two days after this heroic action, he was killed when he volunteered to go on another patrol. His wife, Lillian, was presented with his medal.

On March 6, a motivational rally was held at the Matthiessen auditorium for the employees of Electrical Utilities and Eicor. A crowd of 650, including employees and their families and friends, listened to CPO Harry Semrow explain why 170 million Americans had to "out-produce and out fight" the 450 million Japanese and their conquered subjects. He said, "You production workers are fighting the Japanese as much as your boys at the front. 'Pray, Work, Buy' must be your motto every day as the war progresses." Another speaker, Ensign Barbara Norris, a navy nurse, told the crowd of her impressions of the wounded coming back to San Francisco. She exhorted the audience, "Ask yourselves if you are doing all you can to win the war and resolve once again not to let down for a single moment as long as boys like those over there need your help."

It didn't take much motivation for most Seneca workers to put all their efforts into the war. On March 8, when LST 1132 was launched, Mrs. John Witherspoon of Seatonville was selected as the ship's sponsor. Her husband, John, worked at the Seneca yard for a time before enlisting in the navy on Dec. 7, 1943. He was currently in New Guinea. Her father was a foreman at the yards, and she had 17 cousins in the service!

Children were working constantly to do their part in supporting the home front effort. A paper drive was a simple yet necessary activity that made even the youngest child feel useful. As an incentive in the WPB-sponsored drive, each child was given an armband and a chevron for every 50 pounds of paper brought to school. When the school organized its "Paper Troopers," who would have thought it would be one of the youngest children who would work the hardest. When the final totals were counted, Jack Morrison, 7, a first grader at Central School, was named the champion of the entire Peru school system. During the three-week drive, he brought in 2,631 pounds of paper! His nearest rival was Barbara Hunt, a student at Roosevelt School, who brought in 1,256 pounds of wastepaper.

The Princeton Boy Scouts and Cub Scouts also responded to the WPB's urgent request for additional wastepaper during May. Special recognition was accorded 25 Princeton scouts from Troops 66, 67, and 68, who brought in over 1,000 pounds of paper. Each boy received a bronze medal with the image of General Eisenhower attached to a red and white service bar. *(Note - a similar medal bearing the image of General MacArthur was awarded to children who had outstanding victory gardens.)*

For a serviceman, the next best thing to a letter from home was often a copy of the hometown newspaper. It was one way servicemen could not only read about the scrap drives and ship launchings but also keep track of their friends, who were sent to other areas of the world. One of the favorite features read by both servicemen and residents in the *Putnam County Record* was "Letters From Those in Uncle Sam's Forces." The soldiers could only describe non-military aspects of their duty such as travel to historic places. For instance, Victor Novak wrote about his explorations of Greek ruins while he was in Sicily. Impressive as the ancient ruins might have been, he wrote that he wouldn't trade even the Mark coal dump for anything he had seen overseas. Charles Kassabaum wrote on March 7 about his trip to Rome, where he saw St. Peter's Cathedral. In a letter to Thomas Kennedy, he said, "I find words inadequate to describe what greets the eyes of the visitor. It is truly beautiful."

But the war was not about leisurely visits to historic sites, it was a deadly business. Two months later, in another letter written to the family by an unknown person, it was learned that Kassabaum was badly wounded. The *Record* printed the V-mail letter which ended with the medical assessment that he would be alright in the next few months but, in a cryptic closing, the writer said the soldier would never have to fight again.

Other letters printed in the *Record* gave home front readers greater insights to the actual fighting. Lt. Bud Donaldson, 26, from Granville, was a liaison pilot with the Sixth Army in Luzon, P.I. In May 1945, he wrote. "It is all very exciting and interesting flying over the infantry with two radios, the infantry set and the artillery set, an ear phone in each ear, a microphone on each shoulder, map on one knee, pencil pad on the other, adjusting fire on targets and plotting the patrols and giving them their positions. While all this is going on and trying to fly a plane at the same time, it's all very exciting. Watching the Japs run around madly when we drop down on them with artillery is interesting."

The front page newspaper stories from the front lines in Europe were very positive on April 12. The American 9th Army had crossed the Elbe River and was only 57 miles from Berlin. It was estimated that they were only a day's march from the German capital. The British 8th Army had just punched through the German defenses on the Santerno River in Italy. In the Pacific, the Japanese home islands were being pounded by hundreds of American B-29's. Suddenly, the wire services flashed the news that stunned the nation – President Roosevelt was dead. The Ottawa *Republican Times* ran the headline the next day, "Roosevelt Rites Saturday."

Reaction in the Illinois Valley was swift. In the Tri-Cities, Mayor Orr, Mayor Hasse, and Mayor Pryde issued a joint proclamation asking that all businesses including retailers be closed from 2 p.m. until 5 p.m. on Saturday afternoon. The four major banks in the area closed on Saturday at noon. Flags throughout the Illinois Valley were flown at half mast. Churches held ecumenical prayer services. The Peru American Legion planned to march downtown to Fourth and Peoria Streets and fire a salute at 9 a.m. on Sunday morning.

In Ottawa, Mayor Spurgin requested the closing of businesses from noon to 5 p.m. on April 14. The session of the Circuit Court was adjourned by Judge Frank Hayes until the following Monday. The Roxy, Orpheum, Illinois, and Mars Theaters were all closed until 6:30 p.m. Rev. J.J. Gough, president of the Marseilles ministerial services, announced that, services would be held to pray for both the deceased president as well as newly sworn President Harry Truman.

The next day, at the annual girls' gymnasium exhibition at Ottawa H.S., hundreds of spectators in the stands watched in reverent silence as 425 girls marched on to the gym floor to form a victory "V." One row of girls in evening gowns formed the outside of the letter, and another row dressed in white blouses and shorts formed the inside of the letter. Taps were rendered followed by the playing of the national anthem.

The death of the commander-in-chief caused only a brief lull in the daily determination to win the war. Even the smallest schools continued to contribute to the goal of victory. The students at the Zion Lutheran School in Ottawa were very proud of their Minute Man flag indicating that at least 90 percent of the student body had bought bonds. The flag had been flying at the school since November 1944. The school's 32 children had decided to purchase enough bonds to pay for an army jeep valued at $1,165. Having reached that goal, they decided to take on another project, raising $323 – enough to pay for a machine gun.

During the war years, there had been a number of work stoppages. A shortage of parts for aircraft assembly had prompted management to lay off L-O-F workers at Ottawa. Workers left their jobs in protest, but returned to work on April 12, after an urgent appeal by the navy.

Shortages on the home front were treated as inconveniences of war rather than real hardships. With proper planning and adjustments in buying habits, civilians could cope with the rationing system. Government regulations were simply a fact of life. In mid-April, housewives were informed that OPA applications for canning sugar were finally available at neighborhood grocery stores. The 1945 ration would be 20 pounds per person. No more than 120 pounds of sugar were to be sold to any one family no matter how large it was. The Solid Fuels Administration also informed homeowners to fill out coal applications before May 15. An allotment of 2½ tons of Illinois coal per room was considered the norm in the Midwest. Less coal (1-2/3's tons) was allowed if it came from Eastern coal fields.

Victory seemed to be in sight, but the trains coming through the Illinois Valley continued to be filled with servicemen headed to new assignments. A victorious conclusion to the war required that more troops be sent into harm's way.

So, the Streator canteen was busy as ever in 1945. On April 29, the Seneca Machinists Local 1663 volunteered to man the facility. To feed the hundreds of men that were anticipated for one day, the men had purchased 50 loaves of bread from Kosley's Bakery and 18 dozen doughnuts and six sheet cakes from the W&W Bakery. At the Highland Food Mart, the machinists bought 50 pounds of meat, 15 pounds of sugar, and 24 pounds of coffee. Fresh fruits, consisting of two crates of oranges and a crate of apples, were bought at the Public Food Mart. They also ordered 16 quarts of milk from the Illinois Valley Bakery. Four cartons of cigarettes were purchased from Eby Younger for $5.92. The grand total of the shopping came to $101.71. The union contributed $75, and another $25 was donated by Mr. Sam Carter. The remaining $1.71 came from other donations.

The men began their day at 6:30 a.m. to be ready for the first train. The last of the troops were gone by 10:30 that night. On that single day, they served 1,150 servicemen and women.

Throughout the Illinois Valley, there was a growing realization that the end of the war in Europe was only a matter of weeks away. On May 4, the headline in the Ottawa *Republican Times* read, "All Nazis Quit in Holland, Denmark, Northwest Reich." It was encouraging news, but the country was warned that it was still not V-E Day. More men and supplies were needed to wrap up the fighting in Europe. Seven LST's had been launched in March, and another six LST's were sent down the ways in April to carry the men and supplies to the front.

The construction of LST's to supply the troops continued into the spring of 1945. LST 1142 was moved by three Caterpillar tractors to the launching ways at Seneca.
Our Prairie Shipyard.

LST 1142 was christened by Emily Ekdahl on April 23, 1945.
Photo by F.W. Bazzoni for the US Navy.

LST 1144 received a camouflage paint job before its launching on May 2, 1945. Commissioning did not take place until May 28, 1945.
Our Prairie Shipyard.

    As the Allies moved deeper into Europe, the Germans abandoned their POW camps, and soon, those held captive were coming home. Locally, there was a joyful reunion when Sgt. Harold Foster and Pvt. Edgar Shoemaker returned to Mendota on May 7. They provided detailed descriptions of their POW experiences at the hands of the Germans to the *Mendota Reporter*.

Each man had been in a different German prison camp since being taken prisoner in December 1944. It was hard to forget their confinement in box cars with little to eat. In prison camp, the men were treated fairly well by the Germans with the exception of not having enough to eat. Foster said the prisoners were given only a cup of tea for breakfast. Dinner consisted of a bowl of vegetable soup sometimes containing a bit of meat, which Foster thought was horsemeat. Supper was limited to one loaf of bread to be shared by as many as eight men. Shoemaker was also given horsemeat to eat. With the shortages of fuel for their trucks, the Germans resorted to using horses to pull their artillery. The horses died of exhaustion and were butchered for the POW camps. The only relief came when news reached the prison camp that Patton's army was nearby. The regular German troops abandoned the prisons leaving only old men in charge.

Having survived the prison camps, everyone wanted to know about their ordeal. The Mendota Lions and Kiwanis Club invited the men to describe their experiences.

It was apparent that the Germans were about to surrender, but President Truman had still not made the formal announcement. There was confusion in Ottawa on May 7, when an Associated Press bulletin crossed the newsroom wires stating that the Germans had surrendered. Some churches in Ottawa mistakenly thought this was the official end of the war in Europe and began ringing their bells before President Truman addressed the nation.

In the meantime, plans were made for services in almost every church. The seven Protestant churches of the Ottawa Church Council planned a unity service. The Catholic and Lutheran churches in Ottawa agreed to ring bells in unison to coincide with the president's message the following day. The Zion Lutheran Church planned a special evening service after the official announcement. School was still in session at Ottawa H.S., and a special effort was made by the school's Civic Council to sell additional bonds. A new school sales record of $1,415 was set.

When President Truman finally did announce the unconditional surrender of Germany on Tuesday morning, May 8, he said, "Our victory is but half won. When the last Japanese division has surrendered unconditionally, then only will our fighting job be done." Cities like Chicago took the occasion to have jubilant celebrations, but organizations in the Illinois Valley were more reserved in their reactions. At Wenona H.S., both the teenagers and the grade school children gathered for a patriotic program. Betty Gualandi led the students in reciting the Pledge of Allegiance and singing the national anthem. Other patriotic music and readings followed.

Streator fire sirens were sounded exactly at 8:10 a.m. following Truman's announcement that the war in Europe was officially over. Seconds later, city church bells were rung, train whistles blew, and motorists held down their horns. Businesses and schools closed for the day. In the evening, there were religious services. The Streator *Times Press* reported, "It was a calm and orderly acceptance, in sharp contrast to Armistice Day of Nov. 11, 1918, when the community gave way to riotous demonstrations which continued through the day and far into the night."

In Ottawa, churches tolled their bells, and factory whistles blew. American flags were seen through the downtown business district and in front of many homes. Ottawa churches were filled for the thanksgiving services. The Salvation Army Citadel broadcast a program of speeches and music over its public address system. All businesses, with the exception of a few gas stations, were closed. Movie theaters cancelled shows. The Roxy stayed open but only to sell additional bonds. They were stamped "V-E Day" to commemorate the occasion. It was the first time since the WWII "brownout" was ordered that the marquee on the Roxy was completely illuminated. Most schools stayed in session in Ottawa, but there were brief church services at St. Patrick's, St. Francis' and St. Columba. The public elementary school held patriotic assemblies. At the high school, faculty members made remarks regarding the significance of the day at an all-school assembly. The orchestra played an appropriate selection of music. At 8:30 p.m., Company E of the 5th Infantry Illinois Reserve militia led a parade from the armory to LaFayette Street.

In Marseilles, the sirens were activated for a short time. In keeping with Truman's request that everyone continue at their work, the Marseilles school superintendent directed that the school stay in session with the normal schedule. Mayor Earl Butterfield received mixed responses when he asked some of the businessmen to close at noon. Taverns did not close.

Many workers at the National Biscuit Co. left their jobs following the president's proclamation. Howard Adler, the plant manager, hoped that everyone would be back at their jobs the next day in order to continue full production. National Biscuit products included the manufacture of chip board used for packing artillery shells and the cartons used to pack the K-rations for the troops.

The union workers at Certain-teed Products had agreed with management six weeks earlier that there would be a twelve-hour shut down from 7 a.m. to 7 p.m. whenever V-E Day was made official. Since the president's announcement came after the day had started, work stopped after the message was broadcast.

While some cities "jumped the gun" in celebration, Peru did not sound the siren nor were church bells rung. Mayor Joe Lemier waited for President Truman's official announcement before notifying the police and fire departments that the sirens could be sounded. The schools stayed in session.

In LaSalle, the shrill of factory whistles, coupled with the pealing of church bells and the wailing of the fire department siren, left no doubt that the surrender was official. At LaSalle-Peru H.S., the students marched into the auditorium as Margaret Janz played "Onward Christian Soldiers" on the pipe organ. After Carl Struever announced that the Germans had officially surrendered, the students stood, sang the "Star-Spangled Banner," and recited the Pledge of Allegiance. The program continued with a review of the battles that had taken place since the war began on Sept. 1, 1939.

Typical V-E Day ad in the *Daily Post-Tribune.*

Oglesby's Washington School also held an assembly at which time a silent prayer was offered, and Josephine Smania read the Gettysburg Address. The principal, Miss Kate White, explained the meaning of V-E Day. In addition to the national anthem, the children joined in singing "America the Beautiful," and the girls' chorus sang, "Be Glad You're an American."

The business districts in LaSalle and Peru were swamped by workers who left their jobs at Westclox and Electrical Utilities after Truman's announcement. Eicor closed in Oglesby, and Sampsel Time Controls followed suit in Spring Valley. Utica businesses also closed. Banks closed at noon. Stores that had not opened before the announcement generally remained closed for the day. However, M&H Zinc and the Alpha, Marquette, and Lehigh Cement companies remained in operation. A few students were found wandering around town, hoping to participate in one of the short-lived, spontaneous parades.

Church services were held throughout the Tri-Cities on V-E Day. The Utica Baptist Church held a prayer service. In Oglesby, services were held at the Union Church for its congregation which was joined by the Baptists and members of the Jonesville Gospel Tabernacle. Rev. Wujek held an 8 p.m. service at Sacred Heart Church. The Junior Woman's Club of Oglesby cancelled its regular meeting so that members could attend religious services.

In Bureau County, flags lined the streets in many towns. The *Bureau Country Republican* reported, "Taverns closed, a few merchants shut down their shops, but for the most part, work went on as usual, and Bureau Countians turned uninterrupted thoughts toward the war in the Pacific." In Princeton, a V-E Day audience packed the Princeton H.S. auditorium for a worship service. Hymns were sung, and the chaplain of the American Legion post offered a prayer of thanksgiving.

McCoy Street in Granville was lined with American flags still flying at half mast in memory of the late president when the quietude of the spring morning was broken by the wail of the fire siren at 8 a.m., signaling the end of the war in Europe. Businesses began closing at 10 a.m. Employees, who normally went to Sampsel, Eicor, and Westclox, had the day off.

Some Granville residents attended church services at the Evangelical Lutheran Church. Others went downtown to assist in packing children's clothes for shipment to Europe. Students at Hopkins H.S. listened attentively to Truman's radio address. Following the president's announcement, Principal Roy Pyatt led the students in reciting the Lord's Prayer. The Tri-County track and field meet was held in the afternoon as scheduled. *PC Record,* May 10, 1945.

Truman's victory proclamation was also greeted with somber reverence rather than boisterous celebrations in Mendota. The factory whistles blew and bells rang. There was joy knowing that many soldiers and airmen, who had been languishing in the Nazi POW camps, would soon be coming home, but there was also sorrow as those killed in action would never return. A public thanksgiving service was held in the city park in front of the Mendota library. Ministers from a number of local churches addressed the crowd thanking God for the military and spiritual victory but also noting the fact that the war was not yet over.

One of the immediate effects of V-E Day was the end of 14-week brown-out which had been in effect since Feb. 1. Many businessmen were apparently not aware of the change in WPB policy and continued to keep their advertising lights extinguished on May 7. At dusk on the following evening, the Majestic Theater marquee lights were switched on. Soon, display lights came on at service stations and about half of the downtown businesses.

V-E Day was cause for celebration, but the war in the Pacific continued. Mendotans mourned the loss of S/Sgt. Howard Cromwell, who was awarded the Bronze Star (at right) in February. He was killed in the fighting on Okinawa on April 10. The 35-year old sergeant was to be remembered with the seventh gold star on the service plaque in the Methodist Church.

The thought of millions of refugees in Europe prompted a call from the United Nations for all communities to participate in a clothing collection. The Kiwanis Club in Ottawa took on the organizational responsibility for their city. The Salvation Army opened a clothing drop off station on LaSalle Street, one of many collection sites in the Illinois Valley. By May, the clothing drive organized by the Marseilles' Women's Club brought in 5,500 pounds. Stacks of cartons overflowed at the Mendota canteen on Main Street. Mr. Trout, the Burlington RR agent, quickly realized he would need more than a single box car to load the clothing. The Mendota Boy Scouts volunteered to load the trucks donated by the Conkey Co. and the Mendota Manufacturing Co. Two other trucks were supplied by Mayor Oester and Sam Beetz. It was the combined work of many individuals that made the project such a huge success. The response was tremendous; almost 21,000 pounds of clothing would be shipped overseas. Mr. Chris Serup expressed his gratitude to Karl Erbes for the use of the room over the Kanteen and to Fred Welsch and John Walter, who were in charge of sorting and packing the cartons. The Kiwanis and Lions Club also were active supporters in the campaign. Other towns joining in the clothing collection campaign were Rollo, Compton, and Leland.

Construction of the last LST's were nearing completion in the spring of '45. The shipyard had been awarded five stars for its "E" pennant during the course of the LST contracts. In March, the keels for the last three ships were laid. They would be on the ways for about three months before formal launching.

In June, the Federal Works Agency announced the closing of Seneca housing on June 30. Residents were leaving the Hollywood trailer camp.

The final work was completed on LST 1150 during May 1945.

A large crowd was on hand when LST 1150 slid down the ways. The ship was christened by Marie Sheehan Budd on May 30, 1945. It was used for occupation duty in the Far East in 1945 and finally decommissioned. US Navy photo.

LST 1150 would only be in the water for 21 days for final outfitting after launching. It was not delivered to the navy until June 20, 1945. Later, it was recommissioned the *USS Sutter County*. It was used in the Vietnam War from 1966 to 1970 and was awarded 8 battle stars. US Navy photo.

The mood was somber on June 8, 1945 when Alice Kline christened LST 1152, and it slid down the ways. It was the last of the 157 LST's built for the navy at Seneca shipyard. US Navy photo.

The keel for LST 1152 was laid on Mar. 15, 1945, months before the war in Europe was over. Everyone knew that it was the last navy contract. It was outfitted in 21 days and ready for duty after launching at Seneca on June 8, 1945, but it was not delivered until June 30. It finally arrived in Hawaii on Sept. 8, 1945 – weeks after V-J Day. The ship would never see action in WWII, but was kept in the reserve fleet. In 1955, it was renamed *USS Sweetwater County,* and was eventually transferred to the Republic of China, which renamed the ship the *Chung Ming* in 1958. As of 2002, it was still on active duty with the Taiwanese navy. US Navy photos.

As the navy contracts came to an end, most of the 10,900 Seneca workers had packed their bags and left for other parts of the country. All that remained were a few hundred employees needed to take inventory and move certain equipment to other Chicago Bridge and Iron facilities. The town would soon return to the quiet river community of 1,200 that it had been before the war.
Below: Seneca shipyard identification badge for Erline Houser, Editor of *Our Prairie Shipyard*.

Above: The personnel department at the Seneca shipyard. Seneca library.

More and more servicemen were coming home. "Buzz" Verucchi, a discharged veteran and owner of a bar in Spring Valley, came up with a novel way of remembering his former tavern patrons, who were still in the service. Behind the bar (pictured), he listed the names of 60 servicemen, and next to each name, he posted a flag to indicate each 20¢ donation from his customers. "Buzz" added a nickel to make up the

difference in the price of a 25¢ war savings stamp. When a total of $18.75 in stamps was accumulated, a bond would be bought and held for the serviceman until he returned home.

The 7th War Loan was promoted through the summer of 1945, but citizens had been besieged by so many appeals for additional bonds sales that it became doubtful that the established quotas could be met. To stimulate sales in Marseilles, the Mars Theater manager, P.G. Sklavounis, announced a special 11 p.m. premiere showing of "It's a Pleasure," starring Sonja Henie. It could only be attended by purchasing a bond. The manager stressed the importance of buying an extra bond saying, "There will be the additional expense of planes, guns, and tanks for the tough, long range war against Japan." To assist in the local sales, the Marseilles Boy Scouts, supervised by Richard Rice and Howard Neinaber, visited every house to promote the bonds. The management of the Majestic Theater in LaSalle used the same "free movie" tactic to boost bond sales.

Bond quotas were generally met or exceeded. In Oglesby, Chairman Gildo Costa thanked everyone who helped in any way to sell over $267,000 in bonds, which was $24,000 more than the city's quota. LaSalle's bond sales were over-subscribed by 6% according to Chairman Ken Braun. In Peru Township, Andrew Hebel, the area chairman, expressed his gratitude for the $607,000 in bond pledges saying, "We can all feel proud of the record (118%)."

During the summer of '45, many servicemen returned to tell about their imprisonment in Nazi stalags. Pfc. Leonard Dumke and T5 Robert Wright told Marseilles Rotarians about their ordeal in the POW camps. Dumke said he had to mine 15 tons of coal a day before he was allowed to rest. Wright said, "If it hadn't been for the Red Cross packages we would have died."

Pvt. John Balzarini (at right) of Oglesby told a *Post-Tribune* reporter that he was captured in the Battle of the Bulge on Dec. 19 near Aachen and was almost shot by a firing squad. He also said that American soldiers were denied food during their 10-day trip in boxcars to Stalag 4B in Millburg.

The war was over in Europe, but the fighting became more intense in the Pacific. With tens of thousands of servicemen and women doing their part, workers in the Illinois Valley continued turning out weapons and other necessities of war.

Owens-Illinois continued to manufacture bottles of all types for the government. One of the innovations in manufacturing at O-I was the development of a light-weight beer bottle. While most bottles were refillable, these were non-returnable. The Off-Shore brand was supplied by the Army and Navy as a morale booster. Many of these Duraglas beer bottles were manufactured at the Streator plant. O-I also manufactured medicine bottles for the military.

Line O'Nine, O-I newspaper, June 1, 1945.

The Duraglas bottles turned out at Owens-Illinois in Streator were of the highest quality, a factor which caused some embarrassment to America's First Lady, Bess Truman. On one occasion, she had been invited to christen two new planes, one for the army air force and one for the navy at the National Airport in Washington, D.C. As was the custom in launching ships, a bottle of champagne was to be smashed on the nose of the planes. Mrs. Truman accompanied by her daughter Margaret, stood on the wooden platform along with high ranking military officers.

First Lady Bess Truman with her daughter, Margaret, was ready to christen a new plane. *Line O' Nine,* O-I newspaper, July 6, 1945.

Mrs. Truman was handed a champagne bottle, which had been scored vertically in six places to make sure it would crack easily. The First Lady swung and hit the plane, but the bottle was still intact. She hit the plane again and again – nine times. An army major tried his luck but to no avail. The only damage so far was a dent in the nose of the airplane. The crowd couldn't help but begin to laugh. Finally, a resourceful second lieutenant left the platform and positioned himself just below the nose of the plane. With a hammer in hand, he was ready when Mrs. Truman took one final swing at the plane. The lieutenant struck the bottle and champagne sprayed through the air. The durability of the bottle was traced back to Streator. The Pleasant Valley Wine Co. of Rheims, N.Y., supplier of the champagne, only bought their bottles from the Streator plant.

Photos from *Line O' Nine*, O-I newspaper, July 6, 1945.

Peak employment at GROP had reached over 4,500 in April 1944, but by July 1945, that number had decreased to a little over 2,300. The number of shifts was cut to two on June 18, 1945. Only one shift was needed effective July 2, 1945. However, War Department contracts for shells and projectiles of various sizes required the continued hiring of additional workers at GROP even in the final months of the war.

Job turnover was an ongoing problem at GROP because of the poor air quality and other potential hazards. Mildred Hensler, who worked on Line 2 painting 90mm shell casings, said that there was powder everywhere – it turned your skin yellow. Commenting on the dangers of the job, she said that she had a finger smashed when operating a hoist, which was one of the highest paying jobs at 90 cents an hour. Jane Marshall, a technician in the GROP hospital, said they had many hand and foot injuries. More serious injuries were treated in the Dixon hospital. Some workers, who were filling the shells, were burned by the hot pentolite. Workers on the loading lines were required to have blood tests to make sure that workers did not have low hemoglobin due to the exposure to lead and explosive chemicals. Paulsen, 33, 35, 46.

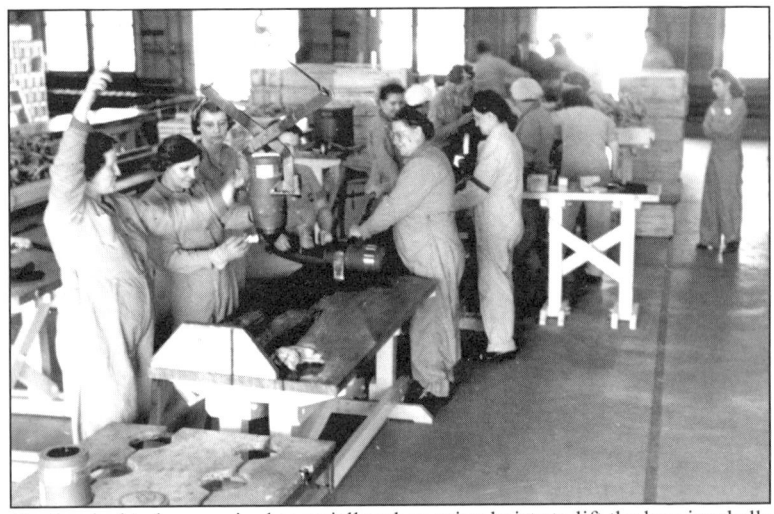

Caution had to be exercised especially when using hoists to lift the heavier shells at GROP. Photo-Paulsen collection.

The Amboy munitions plant produced a large variety of rockets, grenades, projectiles, and shells. These included 57mm, 75mm, 76mm, 90mm, 105mm, and 155mm projectiles, 3-inch, 6-inch, 12-inch, and 16-inch shells, 1000-pound and 1600-pound bombs, bazooka rockets, rifle grenades, and millions of fuses. Production began in October 1942 and continued until August 1945. *Green River News,* Aug. 24, 1945. Ad from the LaSalle *Daily Post* in 1945.

GROP was more than a munitions plant, It was a self-contained community with police and fire departments, as well as a complete medical staff. Workers organized men's and women's bowling leagues, a baseball team, and a 20-member brass band. They held picnics, dances, and cafeteria parties. Paulsen, 21.

Because the workers were not given masks, they were not supposed to be on a loading line for more than six months. Workers are pictured working on projectiles at GROP. Paulsen collection.

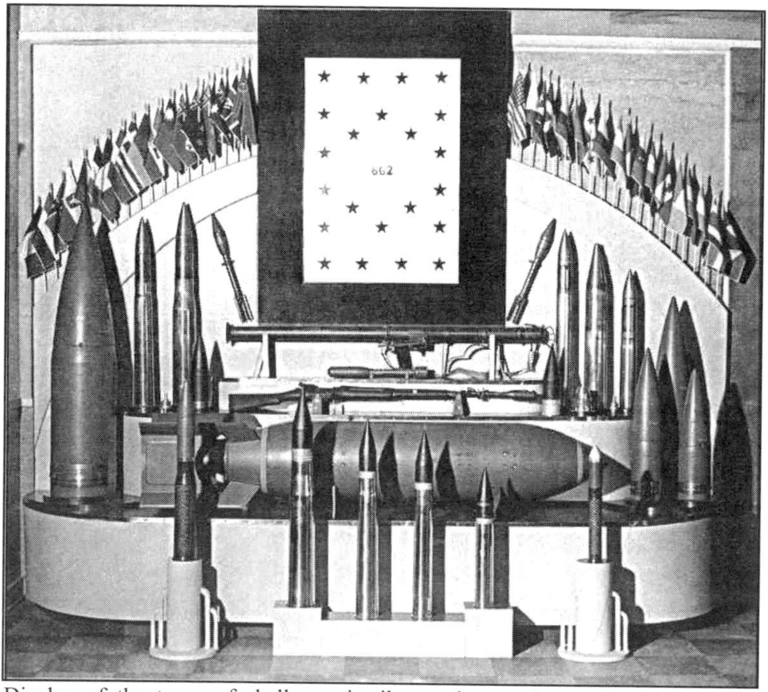

Display of the types of shells, projectiles, and grenades produced at GROP. Paulsen, 1.

GROP employees from different departments were featured in group pictures such as this. One particular group was nicknamed the "Whiz Kids" in recognition of their outstanding production record. Some of the local "Whiz Kids" were Helen Eiten and Marie Prince (Peru), Florence Kalman (LaSalle), Edna Steder (Amboy), Francis Smith (Princeton), Paul Campeggio (Ladd), Pearl Hofeldt and Darlene Croissant (DePue), Peter Kostellic (Granville), and John Springer (Standard). Other "Whiz Kids" came from Dixon, Sterling, and Tiskilwa.

One of the big disappointments for local workers came on July 19 when the Defense Plant Corporation cancelled its plans for a $7 million Inland Tire and Rubber Co. plant located west of Ottawa on Route 6. The operation would have produced truck tires for the military. Two days later, the WPB cancelled its contract for the manufacture of inner tubes at the facility, which was already under construction. Workers already at the job site were simply discharged and told to pick up their checks at the end of the week.

Fund raising projects continued even as the war was drawing to a conclusion. A "doughnut" tag sale was conducted to benefit the work of the Salvation Army in Europe. Mrs. Fred Baum directed the workers in LaSalle, who raised $476. The Oglesby Women's Club turned in $175.

Tin can scrap drives also continued throughout the Illinois Valley in 1945. The government emphasized the need for the old cans which would be recycled into containers needed to protect ammunition, food, and medicine in the jungles of the Pacific islands. Truckload after truckload was brought from Ottawa to the central receiving area in LaSalle. Cub Scout Pack 46 in Naplate collected 700 pounds in one week. The county total for June reached 7,400 pounds.

By the summer of 1945, final victory was not doubted, but no one was quite sure when the Japanese would capitulate. Work on the atomic bomb was known by a select group, and there was doubt in some circles that it should even be used to force an end to the war. With such uncertainties, OPA continued to enforce rationing. The new OPA ration schedule was printed in area newspapers during July and August 1945 so that shoppers knew exactly when, and for how long, certain coupons were valid.

War production may have come to an end at the Seneca shipyard, but Westclox management seemed to indicate that war would drag on indefinitely. On Aug. 7, an ad was run in the LaSalle paper calling for 200 more workers in the fuse department. They were promised a 48-hour work week. "Help Wanted" ads also appeared in the LaSalle paper for additional females 16-45 at Sampsel Time Control.

The bombing of Japan became more intense in the closing days of the war. On Aug. 1, the LaSalle paper reported an attack by 800 B-29's on Nagaoka, Toyama, Mito, Hachioji, and Kawasaki. The next day, 820 American bombers struck again. When the papers reported the dropping of the atomic bomb on Hiroshima on Aug. 6 and Nagasaki on Aug. 9, there was little apparent reaction in the Illinois Valley. The average person only learned that atomic bombs had immense destructive power.

One of the few individuals who had a bird's eye view of the destructive power of the A-bomb was Putnam County's Sterling Anderson. His crew had just finished training with the 313th Wing on Tinian Island in the Marianas, but his bomber group arrived too late to be involved with the Hiroshima or Nagasaki bombing. However, in a letter dated Sept. 6, 1945, he gave the folks back home some indication of the results of the bombing since censorship had ended. Their last mission of the war was flown on August 14 against the Marifu railroad yards. Since it was just south of Hiroshima, the crew had a good look at the destruction. Sterling said, "It was just as bad as published reports." The only other mission he flew after the official end of the war was one to drop aid packages to a POW camp on Honshu.

On Tuesday, Aug. 14, President Truman finally announced that the Japanese had surrendered, and he proclaimed a two-day national holiday. The three years and eight months of sacrifice since the attack at Pearl Harbor had come to an end.

Spontaneous celebrations were seen in every town in the Illinois Valley. St. Joseph's Catholic Church was the first one in Peru to ring its bell to alert the neighborhood of Truman's announcement. Next, the fire siren was sounded for 15 minutes.

In Peru's business district, cars drove up and down the street with horns blowing. Around 9 p.m., Mayor Joe Lemler led an impromptu parade, which included members of the Peru Legion-Municipal Band. They marched down to the Westclox building where a huge sign reading "No Work Wednesday" was hung over the main entrance. Almost every business had posted signs indicating they were closed. At the Majestic and Peru Theaters the signs read, "Victory – We're closed."

Four soldiers in Peru grabbed some American flags located in front of downtown businesses and joined in the parade in their open touring car. Another car packed with teenagers carried German and Japanese flags hanging from the back with a sign reading "This is the End." Other cars jammed with teenagers dragged milk cans, garbage cans, and pails. The downtown area was described as "a sea of vehicles, cars, trucks, and even a few brave bike riders."

Although Sheriff Harbeck ordered the closing of rural bars, the taverns in Peru went "full blast" into the early morning hours. Normal closing hours were not enforced. Residents banged pots and pans in celebration. Small groups of revelers merged to form snake dances that wove up and down the sidewalks and in and out of taverns. According to the *Post-Tribune,* "There were some corners where if you got by without being hugged beyond measure you were lucky and you did not have to be in uniform to get a kiss." Police Chief Joe Potthoff, who ran the department when WWI ended, said, "There were more drunks than the other time." He added, the celebration was "noisy but orderly," but it wasn't necessary to call out the special police.

The scene was similar in LaSalle. Father S.D. Bernardi ran to the Queen of the Holy Rosary Church and rang the bell so enthusiastically that the rope suddenly broke. He had to take a few minutes to repair it so he could continue tolling the bell.

Someone also started ringing the bell in the tower of the No. 1 fire station. It was the first time the bell had been rung in 25 years as far as anyone could remember. At the same time, the sirens at the LaSalle fire station were activated and continued to blast for a half hour. Factory whistles and car horns added to the din.

The police force was changing shift, but the day officers were back on the job after a quick supper. Crowds began forming within ten minutes of the president's proclamation, and cars carrying American flags began parading down the streets. One convertible car carried three servicemen seated high on the back seat each carrying a large American flag. Rolls of toilet paper were thrown everywhere from the cars and out of second story windows. People took to the streets. Hundreds of teenagers were led by a few Legionnaires. Women joined in the foot parade banging their pots and pans vigorously in celebration.

The impact on the phone company was overwhelming for switchboard operators. It was described as a total "blackout." Hardly a call could be connected during the first half hour of celebration as hundreds of residents tried to call their friends to announce the good news.

In Oglesby, a stuffed effigy of Tojo had been dragged through the streets by a car finally coming to a stop so that the city's water and light department truck could extend its ladder to the arm of a light pole. The effigy was tied to the pole with a large placard reading simply "Tojo." Several hundred residents along with Mayor John Pryde and other city officials watched the hanging. Following that, the siren on the police car was sounded, and whistles and car horns were sounded to begin the celebration.

Ottawa had all that and more as guns were fired and bombs exploded. Two ropes were tied to the clapper of the fire bell in front of city office on Lincoln Place. Celebrants kept ringing the bell for hours. Whistles were blown from boats on the river, railroad engines, and the Sanders Brothers factory. Shredded paper floated down as teenagers snake danced through the streets. People from surrounding rural towns came to join in the celebrations. On the corner of Main and Clinton, a barrel of beer was set out and every passerby was offered a free drink. That was of some consolation to those who found their favorite bars had been closed.

Like Oglesby, Ottawa also heaped ridicule on an effigy of a Japanese figure. Here too, Illinois Bell operators worked feverishly to handle the lights flashing on their switchboards.

Hazel Soberri, 17, who was operating the telephone switchboard in Wenona, received word to activate the fire siren to signal the official end of the war. Lights flashed on her switchboard as anxious citizens wanted to know where the fire was. She responded with a curt "The war is over!" Outside, she only caught a glimpse of a convertible full of celebrants racing down the street. She couldn't leave her job manning the phones.

One of Ottawa's servicemen was glad to be in town for the festivities. Lt. James Schmitz, who had been sentenced to death by the Germans, had escaped from his Nazi prison cell in Poland when the American and Russian armies were converging on Germany. He was finally able to return to his home town.

When victory was proclaimed on Tuesday night, Mendota celebrated the news with shouting, singing, and noise making. Churches rang their bells, and factories blew their whistles. Every business closed its doors so that employees could join in the celebrations. The city fire truck led a parade through the streets.

Most residents of Bureau County were eating dinner when Truman's announcement was broadcast. Within an hour, streamers were being thrown into the air covering the joyful crowd on Princeton's Main Street. The wild celebration was punctuated with individuals firing guns into the air and shouting themselves hoarse.

In Putnam County, the story of celebrations in Granville was much the same but on a smaller scale. The old fire bell, which not been tolled in a quarter century was rung. Church bells rang; guns were fired; and car horns sounded long into the night.

Seconds after Truman's 6 p.m. announcement, the news was flashed to the Streator *Times-Press*. The news was then relayed to city hall and Owens-Illinois. Work at businesses and industries quickly came to a complete halt. Impromptu parades of cars – some only a half block in length – began cruising down the streets. The *Times-Press* reported, "By 7 p.m., the business district took on a festive atmosphere. A true carnival atmosphere pervaded and joy was rampant throughout the community." A group of Streator H.S. students hoisted Mayor Thomas Halfpenny to their shoulders and led a parade down Main Street. When uniformed soldiers or sailors were spotted, girls would grab them and shower them with attention until their faces were streaked with lipstick. After parading down the streets, a crowd, numbered in the thousands, gathered at the Santa Fe depot to listen to the Citizens Band. The musical numbers were only interrupted when a troop train came through, and the crowd cheered the men. The festive celebrations continued long into the night as teens and adults alike jitterbugged and snake-danced through the streets. Taverns were closed during the first day of the two-day national holiday but reopened at 6 p.m. on the second day of the celebrations.

At Owens-Illinois, it was time to celebrate. After 6 p.m., only a skeleton crew was kept on the job to maintain the furnaces and other equipment needed for continued post-war production. Work was scheduled to resume on Aug. 16, at 7 a.m. O-I promised discharged servicemen would find their jobs waiting for them, and those who had to remain in the service for a time would also find employment at the plant. Altogether 553 workers or about 40 percent of the traditional workforce had been called to duty; ten paid with the ultimate sacrifice. The *Line O' Nine* listed the Gold Star OnIzers as follows: Ralph Babey, Herman Durree, Elmore Duffy, William Worrell, George Bakalar, Victor Rush, Albert Godfrey, Frank Kozak, Edward Neblock, and Albert Wilson.

Ironically, on V-J Day, a number of army trucks arrived in Streator, but they weren't carrying discharged GI's. The trucks were loaded with German POW's. Men, dressed in ordinary work clothes, went into the Streator Canning Company and Best Foods, Inc. to help can corn and process cucumbers. For the next few weeks, they worked side-by-side with the other cannery workers and said little, although some could speak English. The word got around that they were actually German prisoners who were being quartered in tents behind barbed wire and under guard in a camp on Livingston Road, south of Streator. Twenty American soldiers had been assigned to guard the prisoners and patrol the camp at the old sewer pipe factory of the Streator Clay Co. Lt. Daniel Shultz, the commanding officer of the detail, said that some of the young Germans had been captured when Rommel's Afrika Korps surrendered. The shortage of manpower necessitated the use of the POW's in Streator. Lt. Shultz reassured Streatorites that the prisoners were always orderly and never resorted to an uprising. These same men had performed similar work in Decatur and Hoopestown without any problems. Once the canning season was over, they would be returned to their permanent POW camp at Camp Ellis near Lewistown, IL and eventually returned to Germany.

A victory program was held in Wenona on Aug. 16. Gold Star mothers were honored. The parents of Maj. Edward Kemp and Francis King were on hand, but the parents of the other two casualties, Robert Hill and 2nd Lt. Arthur Strauch, were not available. Congressman Everett Dirkson spoke at the program.

Two days later, its was finally revealed in the *Wenona Index* that Miss Jeanette Artman had been keeping top secret records of A-bomb progress for the scientists at the University of Chicago for a year and a half. It came as a complete surprise to her parents, Mr. and Mrs. James Artman of Wenona.

Layoffs were expected but, the impact at EU in LaSalle was minimal. Although military contracts were cancelled resulting in the closing of some lines, President Al Hauser said, "It is impossible to determine just how many employees may have to be temporarily released, but it would probably not be any large number." The reason was that there was a large backorder for condensers for the civilian market and some navy contracts.

Westclox was also about to make the transition to peacetime production of clocks and watches. The new work schedule was cut back to 40 hours a week. Because of the cancellation of government contracts, it was necessary to send most of the employees home the day victory was declared. Because of the large numbers of employees that were laid off, the U.S. Employment Office in LaSalle was overwhelmed with hundreds of workers seeking unemployment compensation. Rather than have them wait for hours to fill out forms, they were issued a date when they could come back the following week.

OPA announced that all rationing of canned fruits and vegetables, gasoline, and fuel oil would be ended. There were still some commodities that were going to be rationed for awhile, but it was a relief. As OPA Price Administrator Chester Bowles said, "Nobody is happier than we in OPA that the day is finally here when we can drive our cars whenever we please, when we please, and as much as we please."*(Not knowing when the war would end, the OPA had already printed Ration Book Five for distribution in Jan. 1946. Registration for new "A" gasoline books was scheduled to start on Dec. 3, 1945.)*

The Streator chapter of the IOOF took its turn at the canteen in 1945. By its second anniversary, volunteers had served over 1½ million servicemen and women. The average soared to over 2,000 a day – the highest number was almost 5,000. The club continued its work until May 29, 1946. Streatorland Hist Soc.

The end of the war also meant that there would be a transition to a peacetime economy. At the Green River Ordnance Plant, it meant munitions jobs would be gone forever. William Steinwedell, the general manager, said that the plant received notification on Aug. 15 to stop all but a few production lines. He expressed his thanks to the employees for their loyal cooperation during the three and one half years of the plant's operation. Virtually all production came to a halt by the end of the month. The GROP workers arranged a few goodbye parties at the canteen.

Line decontamination was completed by Sept. 1.

On Sept. 2, 1945, Gen. MacArthur accepted the formal surrender of the Japanese government aboard the battleship *USS Missouri*. Chester Nimitz signed the Japanese surrender instruments. Standing from left to right are Gen. Douglas MacArthur, Adm. William Halsey, Rear Adm. Forrest Sherman.

There would still be some temporary work for a few months at GROP. It was necessary to dismantle or destroy some of the buildings. During the months following V-J Day, most of the work at GROP involved taking inventory. The Corps of Engineers was responsible for moving the remaining munitions. Rather than store almost 200,000 pounds of smokeless powder, it was decided to burn it to save money. There wasn't much of a market for gunpowder immediately after the war. The destruction of the powder began on May 21, 1946.

(Note – In the years that followed the war, a variety of industries bought some of the GROP property, but large areas of the deserted facility still remain as a testament to a bygone era. Little remains of the former munitions plant located on Route 30, 3½ miles west of the junction with Route 52. The only reference to the area is a small street sign indicating the location of Corregidor Road. The asphalt road to the administration building is cracked with vegetation slowly engulfing the roadway. Old tires and refuse litter the roadside. The nearby supporting structure (right) for one of the GROP water tanks along Corregidor Road stands like a monument to the thousands of home front workers, whose efforts helped to bring victory to America.)

Left: The roads signs at the site of the old Green River Ordnance Plant are one of the few reminders of the historic aspect of the facility.

Below: Some of the GROP structures used for loading projectiles still have standing concrete walls, but the wooden roofs are gone.
Photos by author.

Private industries have taken over some of the old buildings, but most stand empty. GROP storage buildings, covered with an asbestos-laced siding called transite, are abandoned and surrounded by weeds and junked cars.

Some buildings, were built partially underground with thick, concrete walls, could serve as bomb shelters. They were used as shelters in the summer of 1945 when a tornado threatened the nearby area.

Bunkers, along Corregidor Road, referred to by the workers as "igloos," once held vital supplies of munitions. They are now used by local farmers to store equipment and crops. Photos by author.

    To honor servicemen, a Victory and Constitution Day parade was held in Ottawa on Sept. 16. The Peru American Legion-Municipal band and Peru American Legion color guard and veterans participated. At a 7 p.m. ceremony at King Field, 58 WWII veterans were inducted into the American Legion.

One of the last reminders of the war in the Illinois Valley was seen on Sept 18-19, when Seneca-built LST 512 docked at Ottawa. The ship had been used to supply Patton's 3rd Army, making 30 trips between England and Normandy. Now, it was converted to a floating war exhibit. It was crammed with everything from a Japanese Baka suicide plane to a reproduction of a Pacific jungle complete with a Jap pill box, banyan trees, coconut palms, and a swamp on the main deck. The sounds of jungle animals, pounding surf, and an authentic Japanese Banzai charge added to the realism. Animated maps, dioramas, war souvenirs, and models of various naval craft were also available for viewing. While on tour, the vessel was manned by 200 veterans of the navy, coast guard, and marines. Over 20,000 people visited the exhibit during the two days in Ottawa. LST 512 left Ottawa and cruised by LaSalle-Peru on Sept. 20 on its way to its next port of call, Peoria.

Soon, most of the soldiers, sailors, marines, and airmen would be returning to their homes. Some servicemen brought with them war souvenirs such as this Ten Peso note used in the Japanese-occupied Philippines.

For many, discharge papers meant returning to their farms, looking for new jobs, or returning to old jobs at Westclox, Eicor, or Owens-Illinois. Some men would take advantage of the GI Bill of Rights and continue their interrupted educational pursuits. Many would get married and buy their first home. Even before the war ended, the Eureka Building Association and Peru Federal

Savings were advertising GI Home Loans. The Veterans Administration would pay the first year's interest on the first $2,000 of a home loan, and no down payment was required. Many servicemen remained overseas to occupy the Axis countries.

Veterans of WWII were awarded the Victory Medal (left). Those, who occupied the Axis countries after the war, were awarded the Occupation Medal (right).

Men were still being called by the Selective Service, but the monthly quotas were much smaller. Little did anyone think that another war would break out in a little known country called Korea.